The Common Core
MATHEMATICS
STANDARDS

The Common Core
MATHEMATICS STANDARDS

Transforming Practice
Through Team Leadership

Ted H. Hull ▪ Ruth Harbin Miles ▪ Don S. Balka

A JOINT PUBLICATION

NCTM

CORWIN
A SAGE Company

CORWIN
A SAGE Company

FOR INFORMATION:

Corwin
A SAGE Company
2455 Teller Road
Thousand Oaks, California 91320
(800) 233-9936
www.corwin.com

SAGE Publications Ltd.
1 Oliver's Yard
55 City Road
London EC1Y 1SP
United Kingdom

SAGE Publications India Pvt. Ltd.
B 1/I 1 Mohan Cooperative Industrial Area
Mathura Road, New Delhi 110 044
India

SAGE Publications Asia-Pacific Pte. Ltd.
3 Church Street
#10-04 Samsung Hub
Singapore 049483

Acquisitions Editor: Carol Chambers Collins
Associate Editor: Megan Bedell
Editorial Assistant: Sarah Bartlett
Production Editor: Cassandra Margaret Seibel
Copy Editor: Pam Schroeder
Typesetter: C&M Digitals (P) Ltd.
Proofreader: Caryne Brown
Indexer: Terri Corry
Cover Designer: Gail Buschman
Permissions Editor: Adele Hutchinson

Copyright © 2012 by Corwin

Printed in the United States of America.

Library of Congress Cataloging-in-Publication Data

Hull, Ted H.

The common core mathematics standards: transforming practice through team leadership/ Ted H. Hull, Ruth Harbin Miles and Don S. Balka.

p. cm.
A Joint Publication with the National Council of Teachers of Mathematics

Includes bibliographical references and index.

ISBN 978-1-4522-2622-4 (pbk. : acid-free paper)

1. Mathematics teachers—Training of. 2. Leadership. 3. Mathematics—Study and teaching. I. Miles, Ruth Harbin. II. Balka, Don S. III. Title.

QA16.H848 2012
510.71—dc23   2012003226

This book is printed on acid-free paper.

NCTM Stock Number 14404

12 13 14 15 16 10 9 8 7 6 5 4 3 2 1

Contents

Foldout Pages at the End of the Book

Preface

Improving student success and achievement in mathematics are the goals of this book. The theme is consistent across each of our previous books. In 2009, Corwin released our first book, *A Guide to Mathematics Coaching: Processes for Increasing Student Achievement* (Hull, Balka, & Harbin Miles), which was designed to assist coaches in directly impacting student performance by working with teachers. Within a few months, our second book was released, *A Guide to Mathematics Leadership: Sequencing Instructional Change* (Balka, Hull, & Harbin Miles, 2009). We focused on strategies school leaders could use to increase student success in mathematics achievement. In 2010, we released *Overcoming Resistance to Change: A Guide for School Leaders and Coaches,* and in 2011, Corwin and the National Council of Teachers of Mathematics (NCTM) released our book *Visible Thinking in the K–8 Mathematics Classroom.* Both books specifically targeted classroom instructional change.

Our series of books is based on a study of the research, a review of the literature, and our professional experiences with a combined total of more than 100 years working with school leaders and teachers to improve mathematics achievement. With both our work and our books, we strive to provide school leaders responsible for mathematics achievement, mathematics leaders, and mathematics teachers a practical, sequential process to establish meaningful, significant improvements in mathematics teaching and learning.

Shortly after the release of our first two books, a never before witnessed phenomenon occurred in our nation. A wide-ranging group of state governors (48 of the 50) met to initiate the creation of common content standards. With work completed, the Common Core State Standards (CCSS) were released in 2010. Now, more than 40 states, the District of Columbia, and U.S. territories have signed on to this initiative as work continues and will continue on the assessment portion for many years.

Yet, with the CCSS, school leaders are facing a significant undertaking in transitioning to the new content standards and Standards for

Mathematical Practice. They need more specific help that is directly related to the CCSS than what is contained in our previous books.

With these thoughts in mind, we have written a book for leaders, teachers, and leadership teams that is precise and easy to read, one that selectively pulls ideas from our other books that directly impact leadership concerns and issues. Four different groups of educators need this book:

1. Leaders responsible for mathematics such as principals, assistant superintendents, and curriculum directors;

2. Mathematics leaders such as coaches, specialists, and coordinators;

3. Mathematics teachers; and

4. Leadership teams consisting of representatives from the above three groups.

We are recommending this companion book for all educators responsible for mathematics because it assists them in working collaboratively to understand and adopt the mathematical content and practices. More important, we provide a guide, with supporting forms, for successfully leading the implementation of the eight identified Standards for Mathematical Practice for students that are contained in the CCSS.

Acknowledgments

Corwin is grateful for the contributions of the following reviewers:

D. Allan Bruner, Science and Math Teacher
Colton High School
Colton, OR

Elizabeth Marquez, Mathematics Assessment Specialist
Educational Testing Service (ETS)
Princeton, NJ

Edward C. Nolan, Mathematics Supervisor, PreK–12
Montgomery County Public Schools
Rockville, MD

Sandra K. Peer, Math Educator
Wichita State University
Wichita, KS

Lisa Usher-Staats, Response to Instruction and Intervention Expert
Los Angeles Unified School District
Los Angeles, CA

About the Authors

Ted H. Hull, EdD, completed 32 years of service in public education before retiring and opening Hull Educational Consulting. He served as a mathematics teacher, K–12 mathematics coordinator, middle school principal, director of curriculum and instruction, and a project director for the Charles A. Dana Center at the University of Texas in Austin. While at the University of Texas, 2001 to 2005, he directed the research project "Transforming Schools: Moving From Low-Achieving to High-Performing Learning Communities." As part of the project, Hull worked directly with district leaders, school administrators, and teachers in Arkansas, Oklahoma, Louisiana, and Texas to develop instructional leadership skills and implement effective mathematics instruction. Hull is a regular presenter at local, state, and national meetings. He has written numerous articles for the National Council of Supervisors of Mathematics (NCSM) Newsletter, including "Understanding the Six Steps of Implementation: Engagement by an Internal or External Facilitator" (2005) and "Leadership Equity: Moving Professional Development Into the Classroom" (2005), as well as "Manager to Instructional Leader" (2007) for the NCSM *Journal of Mathematics Education Leadership.* He has been published in the *Texas Mathematics Teacher* (2006)—"Teacher Input Into Classroom Visits: Customized Classroom Visit Form." Hull was also a contributing author for publications from the Charles A. Dana Center: *Mathematics Standards in the Classroom: Resources for Grades 6–8* (2002) and *Middle School Mathematics Assessments: Proportional Reasoning* (2004). He is an active member of the Texas Association of Supervisors of Mathematics (TASM) and served on the NCSM Board of Directors as regional director for Southern 2.

Ruth Harbin Miles coaches rural, suburban, and inner-city school mathematics teachers. Her professional experience includes coordinating the K–12 Mathematics Teaching and Learning Program for the Olathe, Kansas, Public Schools for more than 25 years; teaching mathematics methods courses at Virginia's Mary Baldwin College and Ottawa, MidAmerica Nazarene, St. Mary's, and Fort Hays State universities in Kansas; and serving as president of the Kansas Association of Teachers of Mathematics. She represented eight Midwestern states on the Board of Directors for the NCSM and has been a copresenter for NCSM's Leadership Professional Development National Conferences. Miles is the coauthor of *Walkway to the Future: How to Implement the NCTM Standards* (Jansen Publications, 1996) and is one of the writers for NCSM's *PRIME Leadership Framework* (Solution Tree Publishers, 2008). As co-owner of Happy Mountain Learning, she specializes in developing teachers' content knowledge and strategies for engaging students to achieve high standards in mathematics.

Don S. Balka, PhD, is a noted mathematics educator who has presented more than 2,000 workshops on the use of math manipulatives with PK–12 students at national and regional conferences of the National Council of Teachers of Mathematics and at inservice trainings in school districts throughout the United States and the world.

He is professor emeritus in the Mathematics Department at Saint Mary's College, Notre Dame, Indiana. He is the author or co-author of numerous books for K–12 teachers, including *Developing Algebraic Thinking with Number Tiles, Hands-On Math and Literature with Math Start, Exploring Geometry with Geofix, Working with Algebra Tiles,* and *Mathematics with Unifix Cubes.* Balka is also a co-author on the Macmillan K–5 series *Math Connects* and co-author with Ted Hull and Ruth Harbin Miles on four books published by Corwin.

He has served as a director of the National Council of Teachers of Mathematics and the National Council of Supervisors of Mathematics. In addition, he is president of TODOS: Mathematics for All and president of the School Science and Mathematics Association.

Introduction

There is one predominant theme that is carefully threaded throughout this book: the CCSS for Mathematical Practice. When the K–12 standards development teams established the common mathematics content, they also created a list of standards for mathematical practice. These eight practices are based on research and delineate how students should learn mathematics with meaning. While common mathematics content across state borders is a remarkable achievement with tremendous possibilities, the mathematical practice standards provide the real potential for changing mathematics teaching and learning. These standards are:

1. Make sense of problems and persevere in solving them

2. Reason abstractly and quantitatively

3. Construct viable arguments and critique the reasoning of others

4. Model with mathematics

5. Use appropriate tools strategically

6. Attend to precision

7. Look for and make use of structure

8. Look for and express regularity in repeated reasoning

Most likely, many school leaders will initially ignore these practices while they focus their efforts on content matching and alignment. In the early stages of transitioning, this action is not a problem and actually reflects a sequence we have described in our leadership and coaching books. Leaders need to know how to help teachers carefully analyze and develop a scope, sequence, timeline, and supporting materials for the mathematical content in the CCSS.

Teachers need guidance while studying the content, determining the intended depth to be taught with proper sequencing and clustering of learning objectives into instructional units. Furthermore, leaders need to know to start teachers in a gradual, steady change process. Teachers need to study their grade levels or course content and also the content immediately before and after their grades or subjects. In addition, teachers need to know how to carefully select instructional materials through a process of locating materials that are appropriate, materials that need refining, materials that need developing, and materials that need purging.

During and following this work, the standards for mathematical practice cannot be ignored. The U.S. Department of Education is funding a collaboration of assessment developers to create assessments that target the content but also assess the practices. Once these assessments are put into use, there will be a very high demand for resources that support instruction through the lens of the practices. Our book provides specific tools and recommendations for leaders in meeting this challenge in a practical way.

An additional need for effective leadership is a deeper understanding about how adults change behaviors and beliefs. Our nation has seen decades of reforms directed at improving classroom instruction in mathematics with little sustainable results. The standards for mathematical practice will fall the same way unless leaders actually step out and lead. But they need to know how to lead and how to enact positive change in instruction through shared responsibility and collaboration. We provide specific directions for leadership actions.

THE ORGANIZATION OF THIS BOOK

Our book is arranged sequentially. In Chapter 1, Overcoming Resistance to Change: Four Strategies for Teams, we offer recommendations for leadership teams to be used in implementing the mathematical content and standards for mathematical practice identified in the CCSS. Our belief is that the standards for mathematical practice have a true potential for changing current classroom instructional practices. These standards and the research that supports them are identified and explained in Chapter 2, Transforming Instruction.

With this background information, leadership teams are prepared to initiate work on the four strategies we have identified. Chapter 3, Promoting Adoption and Avoiding Rejection, provides leadership teams with an understanding of adult change. Improvement initiatives in the past have failed due to a lack of understanding concerning adult change. One of the most important factors leaders need to emphasize when working with adults is contained in Chapter 4, Focusing on Students Brings Success. Improvements in instructional methods need to have direct, positive impacts on student learning and achievement.

Chapter 5, Attaining the Common Core Practices, provides and discusses two very important forms for leaders to use in working with teachers and for teachers to use in working with students. These forms help teachers progressively address the Standards for Mathematical Practice. Included in the Appendix are sample problems that demonstrate practices and strategies in action. Chapter 6, Visiting a Transforming Classroom, takes the reader inside a teacher's classroom to see the shift toward implementing the practices. The experience of visiting a fictional but realistic classroom provides leadership team members a rich opportunity to initiate conversations and discuss positive issues and concerns in neutral settings.

Chapter 7, Building Support for Collegial Relationships, presents leadership teams with knowledge concerning issues for sustaining change. While change may be initiated through leadership directives, positive outcomes of the initiatives are not achieved without collegial relationships. Chapter 8, Maintaining Support to Increase Implementation, continues the work of promoting change by providing leaders and leadership teams with methods of monitoring implementation of the CCSS, the standards for mathematical practice, and the progress being made by teachers in this endeavor.

Chapter 9, Leading the Way for Change, alerts leadership teams to some very possible and perilous pitfalls. With the pressure to move forward, leaders may hastily select programs that promise to meet the goals of the CCSS and assist teachers in using strategies that support the practices. Missteps here can have serious consequences for years. Careful analysis of programs before selection is strongly encouraged.

READY-TO-GO RESOURCES

Many practical tools are provided in appropriate chapters. Used as recommended, these tools help focus the work of leaders. We draw your attention to two forms that are in Chapter 5 and also at the end of the book as perforated pullout pages that are of particular importance:

- *Standards of Student Practice in Mathematics Proficiency Matrix* (Figure 5.2)
- *Instructional Implementation Sequence: Attaining the CCSS Mathematical Practices Engagement Strategies* (Figure 5.3)

Implementation of the CCSS in mathematics is a long-term effort. To actually fulfill this promise of hope to our students, leaders and teachers need to understand the purposes and functions of these two forms.

As we noted earlier, the eight standards for mathematical practice identified by the K–12 development teams are contained within the mathematical standards. The practices appear in the introduction to the document and in the overviews of every grade level and high school course content. They are extremely challenging and demand significant changes to the current strategies and approaches used to teach mathematics.

Two issues emerge. First, student practices can be attained only through steady progress over time. Second, teachers, leaders, and students need to shift their thinking concerning mathematics learning with understanding. The two horizontal forms in Chapter 5, concerning a strategy sequence chart and a mathematical practices matrix, provide teachers and leaders with tools for progressively changing instructional strategies. They also supply teachers with indicators of student progress as they gain proficiency in each of the eight practices. The forms work together to guide teachers in a way that makes progress meaningful and manageable for these two complicated issues.

To use these forms appropriately with teachers, and to have teachers and leaders use these forms successfully, leadership teams need to read the chapters preceding the tools as well as the chapters that follow them.

HOW TO USE THIS BOOK

For significant change to occur—change that directly impacts student learning and achievement in mathematics—readers must clearly understand how adults adopt new ideas and change behaviors. Nonetheless, wielding this critical knowledge is of no avail if the factors that need to change are not identified and what the change looks like when implemented is not known. Change is a collaborative process involving large and small group discussions and actions with teachers that are centered on student learning.

The strategies for leadership teams unfold in a definite order with a definite purpose. In order to move forward with the ideas contained in our book, and to do so at a concrete level, leaders and leadership team members should begin with the two forms contained in Chapter 5, which are briefly described in the previous section. Next, readers should carefully read the instructional strategy sequence so the developmental nature of the organization is apparent. With this knowledge, readers study the standards of practice proficiency matrix. This form details what students are supposed to be doing in mathematics classrooms. Finally, readers study the interaction between these two forms.

This background serves as a launch for reading the book in order. Leadership teams now progress through the book and carefully reflect on how each strategy for overcoming resistance to change promotes positive classroom change. School leaders are encouraged to use this book in study-group formats that include representatives from administration, mathematics leaders, and mathematics teachers. To this end, questions are provided at the close of each chapter that can serve as prompts for group discussion. In order to promote successful study groups, identified group leaders will find it useful to read and discuss the book prior to launching more comprehensive study groups.

Leaders who are responsible for mathematics improvement but may not have mathematics backgrounds should not spend undue time with the many mathematics problems contained within the book. These individuals should focus on the intent of the problems but leave in-depth discussions to mathematics leaders and mathematics teachers. Collaboration and coherence are key aspects of successful implementation.

Suggestions and recommendations are provided in this book for creating leadership teams, but each individual school leader will need to adapt and adjust recommendations based on his or her unique situation.

1 Overcoming Resistance to Change

Four Strategies for Teams

In regard to student success and achievement in mathematics, educational institutions have been provided an excellent opportunity to do things differently through careful implementation of the CCMS. One point is obvious; business as usual will produce the same mediocre mathematics results. Without significant change in how things are done, the results are predictable.

Unfortunately, many districts will race to adopt the recommendations with hopes of fixing the learning problem. In reality, this hasty approach will merely address one or more of the many symptoms of the problem rather than the true problem. Time is indeed critical, yet investing up-front time in order to determine the correct path is a judicious move.

The Common Core Mathematics Standards: Transforming Practice Through Team Leadership is specifically designed to help leaders responsible for mathematics instruction as they work jointly with teachers to adopt and implement the CCSS for mathematics and the Standards for Mathematical Practice. Administrative leaders responsible for mathematics are in positions such as principals, curriculum directors, or assistant superintendents. Mathematics leaders are individuals in positions such as coordinators, supervisors, coaches, or specialists. Leadership teams consist of representatives from these two groups plus mathematics teachers. While the two separate designations for leader types are important for change, both will be referred to in our book as leaders.

Principals and other leaders responsible for mathematics must not assume that implementation of the CCSS in mathematics is the sole responsibility of mathematics leaders and teachers. Coordination and cooperation between job duties are essential for success. Successful change comes from coherent and collaborative efforts among school leaders, mathematics leaders, and mathematics teachers. When identifying this collaborative effort, we refer to the *leadership team.*

While undertaking the processes for implementing the Common Core Standards and Standards for Mathematical Practice, our book presents four strategies readers need to know and apply when faced with a change such as the CCSS. These strategies, intended to help overcome system inertia, have been received enthusiastically as we have presented them to various educators across the country. The strategies are:

- Strategy 1: Promoting adoption and avoiding rejection
- Strategy 2: Focusing on students brings success
- Strategy 3: Building support for collegial relationships
- Strategy 4: Maintaining support to increase implementation

A brief description of each strategy is provided as a way for readers to quickly grasp the overall picture of change. Then, each strategy is explained in detail as the chapters unfold.

STRATEGY 1: PROMOTING ADOPTION AND AVOIDING REJECTION

Adoption of a change does not occur without some form of pressure, preferably positive in nature. The exerted pressure to change must exceed the pressure to return to the status quo. In school systems, pressure is applied through monitoring. Leaders responsible for mathematics improvement, mathematics leaders, and mathematics teachers must actually check to see that the requested changes are truly occurring in all classrooms. Monitoring pressure is not punitive or negative but supportive and caring. Recall that all individuals have a learning curve when adopting something new. This learning time is a time for empathy, support, and continued training.

STRATEGY 2: FOCUSING ON STUDENTS BRINGS SUCCESS

The reason to change or adopt an instructional strategy is to improve student learning. This uncomplicated thought is often overlooked when considering changes to classroom structures or actions. The actions of teachers, regardless of the quality, research findings, or purpose of the actions, are of no value if students do not respond in a way that improves learning, understanding, and achievement. Leaders, as well as teachers, make mistakes when they concentrate on teachers' actions and ignore student responses.

This last statement in no way indicates or implies that teacher actions are not vitally important, but the focus needs to be shifted. Rather than document that teacher A did "this," leaders need to document that students responded in a particular way when teacher A did "this." The question then becomes this: Were student responses positive and beneficial? Perhaps this is subtle, but it really is a major point. If the students sit like lumps of clay when a particular strategy is used, it is pointless for leaders to credit teachers with using that strategy or for teachers to assume they are effectively using it.

STRATEGY 3: BUILDING SUPPORT FOR COLLEGIAL RELATIONSHIPS

Peer support during change initiatives is important. Most people find change to be uncomfortable. We establish comfort zones and routines. Consequently, we need to have important reasons to change our routines. This reason is pressure, and it frequently comes from colleagues who are also engaged in the change process. While people do respond to negative pressure, it is not productive in the long term. Adoption involves a willingness to take something on. There needs to be a benefit. Adopting effective instructional strategies requires deeper commitment than compliance. Adoption from positive pressure arises from rapport, relationships, and trust.

Teachers work in isolation for significant parts of their days. However, isolation is one of the greatest impediments to enacting change. Alone in a classroom faced with 30 students, the teacher must make an enormous leap of faith to try something new if what he or she has done appears to be working. In most cases, *working* means the students are under reasonable control, the teacher is managing the classroom, and mathematics material is being covered.

If change initiatives driven by the CCSS are to actually improve classroom instruction, isolation must be removed. Teachers need to have opportunities to talk and share with other adults about the strategies and the results of the strategies. Direct, in-classroom support works best for initiating, honing, and adapting new instructional strategies.

STRATEGY 4: MAINTAINING SUPPORT TO INCREASE IMPLEMENTATION

When working with change initiatives, educators often confuse or misunderstand how adults adopt and adapt to change. Leaders, for instance, frequently think of schools as very large buses. They see the job as getting everyone on the bus, and then it is the job of the bus driver (professional development provider or mathematics leader) to get teachers to the correct destination. In response to this idea, teachers are sent to large group training sessions, provided new information, and then released to return to their individual classrooms ready to make the requested changes. As a general rule, this approach does not appear to have any form of positive success record. The training is done to teachers rather than with teachers.

These processes are often the direct opposite of schools' traditional approaches to managing change initiatives. Leaders, working with teachers, need to know how to methodically build critical masses of support for the changes that will occur with the mathematics content standards and the Standards for Mathematical Practice in place.

Finally, leadership for change must be deeply considered. Change is most effective when managed by a principal and a small group of educators who serve as a cohesive force (Marzano, 2003; Reeves, 2006) while working toward developing a critical mass of adopters. In order to build this critical mass, the sequential progression of our book is identified in the box that follows. While we encourage readers to progress through the book as written, identifying the purpose of the chapters will allow readers to focus on or reread particular areas of interest.

Chapter Purposes	
Overview of Strategies	Chapter 1
History and Development of Mathematical Practices	Chapter 2
Strategy 1: Promoting Adoption and Avoiding Rejection	Chapter 3
Strategy 2: Focusing on Students Brings Success	Chapter 4 Chapter 5 Chapter 6
Strategy 3: Building Support for Collegial Relationships	Chapter 7
Strategy 4: Maintaining Support to Increase Implementation	Chapter 8
Common Errors in Program Selection	Chapter 9

QUESTIONS FOR DISCUSSION

How are leadership roles differentiated in your school?

How do leadership roles overlap?

Do leaders and teachers share a consistent message about student learning?

When considering the four strategies, what are some critical elements of each?

How do leaders or teachers overcome isolation in your district?

2 Transforming Instruction

The CCSS came into existence in 2010 through a joint effort of the National Governors Association Center for Best Practices (NGA Center) and the Council of Chief State School Officers (CCSSO). Many stakeholders were involved in writing the standards. The NCTM monitored the drafts and provided continuous feedback to the NGA during the writing process. As noted in the preface of the NCTM (2011, p. ix) publication *Making It Happen: A Guide to Interpreting and Implementing Common Core State Standards for Mathematics,* NCTM supported the goal and intent of the CCSS, which focus on work that the Council had previously done.

According to the development teams, the standards:

- Are aligned with college and work expectations;
- Are clear, understandable, and consistent;
- Include rigorous content and application of knowledge through high-order skills;
- Build on strengths and lessons of current state standards;
- Are informed by other top-performing countries so that all students are prepared to succeed in our global economy and society; and
- Are evidence based (from http://www.corestandards.org/about -the-standards).

By implementing the CCSS, we have the prospect of ensuring equity and access to high-quality mathematics for every student. By accepting standardized mathematics content that spans state borders, we have established a high level of expectations for our students. This step alone will have a significant impact on education.

Having stated that, the common content aspect of the CCSS is minor when compared to the possibilities that exist for the other significant part of the initiative—the eight Standards for Mathematical Practice identified by the developers and adopted by the joining states. The practices draw upon research that strongly supports active student engagement in the classrooms as well as learning with meaning (National Research Council, 2004). Educational leaders responsible for mathematics education must grasp this opportunity and work to ensure that it becomes reality.

The challenge for school leaders, mathematics leaders, and mathematics teachers alike will be to achieve clarity of understanding about the eight student practices and then to transfer this understanding into classroom actions related to instruction. The practices strongly indicate both how students should learn mathematics and how students should demonstrate their understanding. This dynamic shift from telling students about mathematics to having students experience mathematics cannot, and will not, occur without strong leadership.

THE NATIONAL COUNCIL OF TEACHERS OF MATHEMATICS PRINCIPLES AND PROCESS STANDARDS

More than a decade before the new CCSS were developed, NCTM (2000) released its *Principles and Standards for School Mathematics,* providing clarification of six principles and five process standards essential to effective mathematics instruction. NCTM's six principles are *equity, curriculum, teaching, learning, assessment,* and *technology* (p. 11). They are not specific to mathematics but are important to improving and sustaining an effective program:

- *Equity:* High expectations and strong support for all students
- *Curriculum:* Coherent, focused, and well-articulated curriculum
- *Teaching:* Understanding, challenging, and supporting student learning
- *Learning:* Student learning with understanding, actively building new knowledge
- *Assessment:* Useful information to both teachers and students from assessment data
- *Technology:* Use of technology that enhances student learning

In conjunction with these principles, NCTM (2000) identified five process standards to guide classroom instruction and student learning in mathematics. These five process standards are (p. 7):

- *Problem solving:* Use a variety of strategies, reflect on the results, and transfer to new situations
- *Reasoning and proof:* Make conjectures and provide justifications for one's thinking

- *Connections:* Continue to build and expand understandings of mathematical systems and how the systems operate together
- *Communication:* Organize one's thoughts, listen and evaluate others' thinking, and use appropriate vocabulary
- *Representation:* Model mathematical situations in various ways, transition between words and symbols, and interpret mathematical symbols.

HOW ARE THE NATIONAL COUNCIL OF TEACHERS OF MATHEMATICS AND COMMON CORE STANDARDS RELATED?

The CCSS identify eight standards of practice. These practices delineate what students should be able to do in mathematics in order to learn with understanding and what teachers should focus on as they teach content. The eight practices are listed below. As NCTM has described, these eight practices intersect with all five of the Council's process standards as shown in Table 2.1. The practices, more than the content, are what make the CCSS essential for student success.

1. **Make sense of problems and persevere in solving them.** Mathematically proficient students start by explaining to themselves the meaning of a problem and looking for entry points to its solution.

Table 2.1 NCTM Process Standards and the CCSS Mathematical Practice Standards

NCTM Process Standards	CCSS Mathematical Practices
Problem Solving	1. Make sense of problems and persevere in solving them. 5. Use appropriate tools strategically.
Reasoning and Proof	2. Reason abstractly and quantitatively. 3. Critique the reasoning of others. 8. Look for and express regularity in repeated reasoning.
Communication	3. Construct viable arguments.
Connections	6. Attend to precision. 7. Look for and make use of structure.
Representation	4. Model with mathematics.

Source: Implementation of the Common Core State Standards (2010).

2. **Reason abstractly and quantitatively.** Mathematically proficient students make sense of quantities and their relationships in problem situations.

3. **Construct viable arguments and critique the reasoning of others.** Mathematically proficient students understand and use stated assumptions, definitions, and previously established results in constructing arguments.

4. **Model with mathematics.** Mathematically proficient students can apply the mathematics they know to solve problems arising in everyday life, society, and the workplace.

5. **Use appropriate tools strategically.** Mathematically proficient students consider the available tools when solving a mathematical problem.

6. **Attend to precision.** Mathematically proficient students try to communicate precisely to others.

7. **Look for and make use of structure.** Mathematically proficient students look closely to discern patterns or structures.

8. **Look for and express regularity in repeated reasoning.** Mathematically proficient students notice if calculations are repeated and look both for general methods and for shortcuts (Common Core State Standards, 2010).

If students are engaged in these practices, then they are learning meaningful, quality mathematics. The job of leaders is to ensure NCTM principles are addressed, the CCSS content is taught, and most critically, the mathematical practices are attained in every mathematics classroom. The following chapters guide leaders in the process of putting all the pieces together into an effective program in which all students are successful.

Great efforts were made to include a broad spectrum of interested parties as the standards were written. The development teams incorporated many, but not all, of the numerous suggestions offered for mathematics content and mathematical practices. Now, our task as leaders and as teachers is to implement their work.

What Needs to Change?

Leadership teams need specific advice and recommendations concerning resistance to change, and we will address the elements related to adult change—the *how* of effecting change in schools and districts—in the next chapters. First, however, team members need to understand the factors or *whats* they are to change and the related categories.

Using the NCTM (2000, p. 11) principles, leadership teams have a starting point for organizing the elements needing change as they implement the CCSS. They provide an excellent framework for leaders to use in guiding comprehensive change.

Equity. Leaders and teachers need to renew their focus on all students being successful. When inequities are discovered in performance, change initiatives are investigated and implemented without seeking to offer excuses or place blame.

Curriculum. Leaders and teachers need to ensure proper content focus. They need to ensure that appropriate CCSS mathematics content is added as well as ensure that inappropriate content is removed from courses or grade levels. These changes have direct impacts on classroom learning objectives as related to both content depth and concept connections. Leaders will direct the work on a new scope, sequence, and timeline. Instructional materials and resources will be carefully analyzed for appropriate CCSS content.

Teaching and Learning. Leadership teams need to monitor changes in classroom instructional strategies to ensure the strategies being used actually reflect the intent of the mathematical practices. Students must become much more active and engaged in mathematics lessons.

Assessment. By understanding the purpose of the mathematical practices, leaders and teachers ensure that the assessments used to indicate student learning actually reflect learning and understanding of mathematical skills and concepts. In order to do this, assessments must be varied to include individual, group, open-ended, and rubric-scored tasks. Leaders also help teachers carefully analyze the various assessment data to inform both teaching and learning.

Technology. Leaders and teachers carefully check to ensure technology is being appropriately utilized in classrooms to enhance and extend learning opportunities for students.

As a quick review, the boxed list that follows provides bulleted points for each NCTM principle.

The CCSS Whats to Change for Leaders

Equity

- Renewed focus on all students
- No excuses or blame

Curriculum

- Mathematics content
- Learning objectives
- Instructional units
- Scope, sequence, and timeline
- Materials and resources

Teaching and Learning

- Instructional strategies
- Mathematical practices
- Student engagement

Assessment

- Variety of types
- Critical analysis of data
- Informs teaching and learning

Technology

- Facility in use
- Extends learning

A glance at this list prompts the realization that mathematics education has proved extraordinarily resistant to change; many of the *whats* identified in this list have remained static for decades. Regardless of the most recent initiative or call for actions such as No Child Left Behind, daily classroom routines have basically remained steadfast. School leaders have attended hundreds of meetings and trainings. Mathematics teachers have attended hundreds of hours of professional development. In spite of this exposure to new knowledge, change has not occurred in a vast number of school districts. Now, once again, an incredibly massive and encompassing initiative, backed by more than 40 states and the federal government, is facing school and classroom doors. Will the CCSS initiative be successful where others have failed? The answer is a definitive . . . well, maybe.

QUESTIONS FOR DISCUSSION

How did the Standards for Mathematical Practice evolve over time?

Compared to previous work on teaching and learning, how are the Standards for Mathematical Practice different?

3 Promoting Adoption and Avoiding Rejection

As educators read this book, they may be wondering how schools and classrooms have managed to be resistant for so many years against significant pressures that have been exerted. This lack of change appears almost incredible. Can resistance to change really be that persistent? Yet the fact remains that long-lasting change in mathematics that profoundly impacts student learning has not happened. Is it possible to identify a consistent pattern to this lack of change?

After some reflection and reviewing the factors (or *whats*) and categories of schooling that have not changed, readers probably realize that professional development training for teachers is intended to address many of these. However, like classroom instruction, professional development has been offered in much the same way for a significant number of years. Perhaps the approach being used to encourage teachers to change classroom instructional strategies does not match how adults change. The typically cited problem—resistance—may not be the issue at all.

In the scenario that follows, we offer an all-too-common unfolding of events that illustrates how the best of intentions with regard to professional development can go awry. The reasons become apparent only after the effort has failed to achieve the desired results.

SCENARIO 1: THE UNADOPTED PLAN

An elementary school principal realized her teachers were teaching mathematics in the same way that she learned mathematics as an elementary student quite some years ago. She was never strong in mathematics but studied hard and managed to do fairly well in her required mathematics courses in high school and college. In her years of experience as a teacher, assistant principal, and now principal, she knew there were certainly more effective ways to teach mathematics.

She set up a meeting with her grade-level leaders and expressed her concerns about mathematics teaching and learning. For the most part, her grade-level leaders were understanding and somewhat willing to do things differently, but they really did not know what to do. The principal asked if the grade-level leaders would be willing to receive advice and recommendations from a mathematics education expert if she could locate someone to come in. The leaders agree that they would be willing to listen to the mathematics education expert.

At the next district principals meeting, the elementary principal asked her colleagues if they knew of anyone who could help her teachers with mathematics. The principal was given the name of an individual who had presented a session at a professional meeting one of the other elementary principals had attended. "She is young, enthusiastic, and definitely knows her stuff," stated the colleague.

The principal contacted the mathematics education expert, arranged for a day, provided release time for her grade-level leaders, and set her plan in motion. The grade-level leaders were originally concerned about the expert being so young, but after a brief period of time, they began to warm up and gain real enthusiasm. The expert pulled out game after game and activity after activity for the teachers. The expert explained supporting strategies for the various games, such as collaborative grouping, higher-order questioning, wait time, prompts and cues, rubric scoring, sharing thinking, discourse, and journal writing.

Before leaving for the day, the expert worked with the teachers to design a plan for implementing the strategies during the course of the year. The principal was invited to review the plan and was ecstatic about the ideas. The teachers had a schedule for implementing a new strategy every two to three weeks based on their content scope and sequence and benchmark tests.

The principal asked her teachers to remain after school one day for training. She told the teachers she knew this was a lot to ask, but she would provide pizza and even child care for those who needed it. The principal explained that the grade-level leaders needed to train all the teachers in the new plan for utilizing instructional strategies. The training was held and actually very successful. The teachers liked the recommended games and activities.

The next benchmark assessment was only two weeks away, so the principal disregarded the reports because the teachers did not have sufficient time to implement the strategies. She eagerly awaited the next benchmark assessments given during the following six weeks. When she received her scores, she was stunned. The scores were actually lower than in previous years. The principal knew about learning curves and potential dips in scores when first implementing something new, so she hid her disappointment, as well as the scores, and waited for six more weeks.

Again, the scores were not very good. They were better than the previous six weeks and almost up to the scores for the same period last year. The principal was stumped. Then she remembered one of her elementary colleagues in a school whose campus did not make adequate progress and was on an improvement plan. The plan included a mathematics coach. The principal called her colleague and stated that she knew her request was unusual, but she was desperate. Could she please talk to the mathematics coach? Her colleague agreed, and the mathematics coach agreed to visit with the principal after her contract time ended at 4:00 p.m.

At 4:15 p.m., the mathematics coach arrived. The principal immediately began telling the coach her story concerning instructional change. She just didn't know what to do. The strategies were effective; weren't they? The expert was correct, right? The experienced mathematics coach listened carefully until the principal was finished.

The mathematics coach stated that she felt she could help, but the principal had to promise to do exactly what the coach asked her to do with no exceptions. The principal readily agreed. The mathematics coach restated that she was very serious and the principal had to give her word; otherwise, the mathematics coach would not help. The principal was taken aback, but she promised.

The mathematics coach said that she wanted the principal to visit every mathematics classroom over the next two days, and she should visit the same classrooms more than once. She provided her with the following instructions:

1. Enter the classroom, and stand just inside the door.

2. Greet the teacher, but do not interrupt the lesson.

3. Stay for three minutes, and then go to the next classroom.

4. Do not take any notes in the classroom.

5. If you observe one of the games or activities, make a note after leaving the room about the time, grade level, and game.

6. If you observe one of the instructional strategies, make a note after leaving the room about the time and grade level.

7. You are not allowed to talk to any of your teachers about what you observe.

The coach reminded the principal of her promise and indicated that she would return at 4:15 p.m. on the second day. The principal did exactly as asked. She was puzzled and confused, but after all, she was the one who had asked for help. Anyway, what could it hurt? She should have been in classrooms before now.

The principal began her day by entering mathematics classrooms. As mathematics was taught at different times for different grade levels, getting into the rooms was actually easy. She entered the first room, one of her grade-level leader's, stayed three minutes and left. She had nothing to write down but wasn't concerned. She continued her visits. When she was on her second round of visits, she had only noted seeing two of the games. The students were playing the games with partners as the teachers graded papers.

The principal stopped going to rooms before she had finished the second day. She was devastated. Her teachers had really played her for a sucker! She trusted them. She even had a signed copy of the strategy agreement in her office. She was ready to explode. The temptation was almost too much, but she had given her word. She just had to wait until after she finished talking to the mathematics coach.

At 4:15 p.m., the mathematics coach arrived. She entered the principal's office and closed the door. Before the principal could say anything, the mathematics coach said, "I bet you don't have very much if anything written in your notes. I will be actually surprised if you saw even one of the strategies being used."

The principal was so stunned that she forgot she was angry. The mathematics coach continued, "I know you are probably furious with your teachers, and you are feeling betrayed. You need to understand that this isn't anyone's fault. What your teachers told you they would do, they seriously intended to do. The mountain was just way to steep, and they have no climbing gear."

As the mathematics coach continued, the principal realized what she had done. The mathematics coach reminded the principal that the teachers had not been trained in the strategy and did not know how students were supposed to react to the strategy, much less how the strategy would improve learning. They barely had time to think about the strategy before another one was to be adopted. They did not understand the purpose of the games, and the content alignment of the games had not been checked against content standards, much less the benchmark schedule. In other words, the teachers had been superficially involved, not well prepared, and had received no support. The plan had been unrealistic and doomed to failure before the ink was dry.

Reflection

Rejection of a change request, as in the preceding scenario, is far more common than *resistance* to a change. Generally, teachers are not by nature resistant to school authority. Given proper training and support at the appropriate time, as well as opportunities to be involved in the decision-making process for a change initiative, almost all teachers will adopt a change. Leaders must remember that teachers adopt change in small groups. They must be strategic about how to foster the adoption.

HOW ADULTS CHANGE

Within a community such as a school, adults have a consistent pattern for adopting change (Rogers, 1995) and a consistent pattern for mastering the change once adopted (Hall & Hord, 2001). There are basically three groups that form once a change has been proposed and adoption of the change has been accepted. These groups are initiators, earlier adopters, and later adopters (Hull, Harbin Miles, & Balka, 2010). Initiators will generally start the requested change immediately and consist of about 3% to 10% of the community. Following these initiators are the earlier adopters who make up about 5% to 20% of the community (Rogers, 1995). Earlier adopters are not really influenced by the actions of initiators. Rather, earlier adopters realize the benefits of the change and begin adopting. Following earlier adopters are the later adopters. This group is completely influenced by earlier adopters' actions and consists of about 75% to 80% of the community population.

Once a group (initiators, earlier adopters, or later adopters) has adopted the requested change, each person in the group experiences a learning curve as he or she moves from novice to mastery to expert. Hall and Hord (2001, p. 82) cite a University of Texas study in which they offer a Levels of Use of the Innovation progression (see the boxed list that follows). However, that significant first step—the adoption—can be the catch that derails the entire process. What happens when the change is not approved or adopted?

Levels of Use of the Innovation	
U	VI Renewal
S	V Integration
E	IV B Refinement
R	IV A Routine
S	III Mechanical
N	II Preparation
O	I Orientation
N	0 Nonuse
U	
S	
E	
R	
S	

Source: Loucks, S. F., Newlove, B. W., & Hall, G. E. (1975). In *Measuring Levels of Use of the Innovation: A Manual for Trainers, Interviewers, and Raters* (pp. 171–195). Austin: The University of Texas at Austin, Research and Development Center for Teacher Education.

Adults change, or adopt change, when there is sufficient pressure applied to support the change processes. In cases where there is no pressure, most adults merely reject or ignore the change request and remain with their current behaviors. Rejection is a serious problem and a direct result of the traditional approach to professional development and lack of teacher involvement. Teachers reject change when they return to their classrooms after training in which they have no vested interest and face their current circumstances. Regardless of the intent, teachers in their current classroom conditions usually counter change momentum because the pressure and needed support are too little or nonexistent. Leaders also adopt change through the same process. Frequently, routine requests are ignored until sufficient pressure is applied.

Overcoming resistance to change mostly consists of removing opportunities to reject it. Resistance does rarely occur, but leaders need to clearly consider where they need to spend their energy. If leaders cannot get a critical mass of nonresistant teachers to adopt a change (at least 85%), why be concerned about the few possible resisters?

Earlier in this chapter, we posed a question regarding success or failure of the CCSS initiative. We asked if this initiative was also doomed to failure just as numerous others have. Our answer was, "Well, maybe." The *maybe* resides with the will and desire of leaders to actually take defined and purposeful steps to lead. Success or failure of the CCSS does not reside with teachers but with the individuals responsible for providing leadership to teachers in this change process. In this book, we offer four strategies for overcoming resistance, which actually means overcoming rejection. The first of these—and the focus of this chapter—is fostering adoption.

FOSTERING ADOPTION

Every action taken to promote adoption diminishes both rejection and resistance. By considering the information concerning initiators, earlier adopters, and later adopters, leaders realize they may need to change their mental images or models of their schools. Teachers can no longer be viewed as riders on a large bus, and leadership can no longer be viewed as getting everyone on the bus. Further, leadership for change does not reside with one individual.

The large bus model is actually more like a four-door sedan. The leader can get only three or four adults, plus the driver, in the car at one time. Now, leaders must use leadership skills to carefully consider whom to take in the car, in what order, and to what destination. The leader must continually shuttle the teachers to the destination. The good news for leaders is that others can be allowed to drive, but the leader, supported by leadership teams, must know the destination and provide clear directions.

Continuing this analogy and combining it with the information on adult change, leaders find that the initiators, after training, have jumped into whatever vehicle is available and are already moving toward the destination. The bad news for leaders is threefold. First, teachers who are not initiators do not get into a vehicle and do not follow the initiators. Second, without monitoring, initiators may miss the intended destination. Third, the individuals who need to be driven to the destination first are the earlier adopters. If earlier adopters—formal and informal teacher leaders—do not get in the car and go to the destination, later adopters (a large majority of the staff) will not ever get into the car.

Consequently, leaders, with input from teachers and staff, must be able to sort their teachers. Sorting decisions are based on teacher comfort or interest in the change. This categorization is not negative but based on human nature and the current conditions. Later adopters are generally as effective as earlier adopter teachers and certainly as effective as initiators. When teachers adopt a change is no indicator of classroom effectiveness. As leaders consider change, they need to first determine if the change directly and positively impacts student learning. If so, then they need to work to get their earlier adopters engaged and involved in the change process by forming leadership teams.

We have provided a Levels of Adoption form (Figure 3.1) to assist leaders and teachers in organizing their thoughts about teachers who may serve on a leadership team. This organizational template is a starting place that can assist leaders in a process of reflecting on their teachers' willingness to initiate change.

USING THE LEVELS OF ADOPTION FORM

Successful implementation of the CCSS will take time. Implementation could be viewed as climbing stairs. Each successive step up brings individuals nearer their goal of reaching the top of the stairs. Annual campus or school strategic plans should consider which step is the next one up and how leaders and teachers should take the next step.

Within our book, we offer two critical stages toward adoption. First, teachers and leaders are engaged, and then teachers and leaders are empowered. Engagement occurs in the early stages of adopting change and is related to the learning curve identified by Hall and Hord (2001) in Figure 3.1. Empowerment arises in the later stages of adoption and is related to proficiency or mastery of the change. When considering rejection, leaders can clearly see that, if teachers never enter the engagement

Figure 3.1 Levels of Adoption

List Individuals and Actions

Innovation being adopted _____

Use this form periodically to measure progress of adoption.

Initiators	actions	Earlier Adopters	actions
3–10%		15%	

Actions (pressure) you and others are exerting

Actions (pressure) you and others are exerting

Later Adopters	actions	Resisters	actions
60–82%		15%	

Actions (pressure) you and others are exerting

Actions (pressure) you and others are exerting

Active rejection
Passive rejection

Source: Hull, Harbin Miles, & Balka (2010, p. 103). Reprinted with permission.

stage, they will certainly never reach the empowerment stage. Also, leaders realize that teachers must be supported throughout the engagement stage in order to gain sufficient mastery of the change if teachers are to reach the empowerment stage. In addition, if leaders do not engage in required actions, they will not achieve empowerment with change initiatives.

As readers review the Levels of Adoption form, they observe four quadrants: initiators, earlier adopters, later adopters, and resisters. When they think about individuals on their staffs, they want to decide where each individual is most likely located within the first three quadrants. There are no resisters in the first iteration of the form because no actions by leaders have occurred to apply pressure for change. If the change initiative has already been launched, then all four quadrants are used.

There are some general guidelines that leaders and teachers assisting in formulating leadership teams should consider:

- Write in pencil; first impressions can be wrong.
- Individuals shift categories based on the change request.
- No value is attached to a person's category.
- List no resisters when first starting the process.

As suggested, leaders and selected teachers complete the form in pencil prior to initiating training on the identified change. After the first training, leaders and teachers want to revisit the form, walk around various classrooms, and consider the accuracy of their first impressions. At this point in time, leaders are not particularly interested in initiators, later adopters, or potential resisters. Leaders and teachers want to identify earlier adopters. These formal and informal teacher leaders are the key to success. If research is correct, and we believe it is, then change initiatives will not be effective without the support of earlier adopters. Leaders must note that, following the first training, only initiators tend to employ the strategy or innovation.

Leaders and assisting teachers need to be willing to directly ask earlier adopters for their support and assistance in using the innovation or strategy and participating in a leadership team. As earlier adopters begin the process, they can be used to help later adopters form teams to begin the adopted change. After training has started and monitoring begun, leaders want to revisit the Levels of Adoption form and make necessary adjustments. As a reminder, the Levels of Adoption form provides guidance to leaders and leadership teams concerning where to spend their time and energy for initiating and sustaining change. The form does not, nor is it intended to, identify effective or ineffective teachers.

Leaders may find it useful to seek additional sources of opinion about earlier adopters by talking to individuals who may have visited classrooms or worked with teachers. These individuals may include mathematics coaches, specialists, coordinators, or curriculum directors. Leaders may also ask their entire staffs. An easy way to do this is to have teachers respond to a few questions created by the leaders and selected teachers. Responses may be formally written or informally discussed. Answers to the questions are used by leaders to verify their own ideas about who is an earlier adopter.

If leaders do decide to ask all teachers, they should take very seriously the responses even if they contradict the leaders' opinions. Questions may include:

- If you have questions concerning school policy, then whom do you ask?
- If you have a question concerning classroom management, then whom do you ask?
- If you have a question concerning school activities or schedules, then whom do you ask?
- If you have a question concerning instructional strategies, then whom do you ask?
- If you have a question concerning course (or grade-level) content, then whom do you ask?

When asking teachers to complete these questions, leaders should encourage them to consider only naming their top two selections per question. Also, leaders want to get immediate reactions to the questions, so teachers should be provided only a brief period of time to respond. Finally, leaders need to consider the questions. Different teachers may have perceived talents, so leaders want to match the earlier adopters to the anticipated change.

The questions are specifically broader than the desired information leaders are seeking. For work around implementing the CCSS, leaders are interested only in the last two questions involving strategies and content. The additional questions are included to help leaders determine a broader social network utilized by various teachers. In all likelihood, the teachers most frequently identified for strategies and content are informal or formal leaders and are the earlier adopters.

After working with the form and initiating change, leaders may discover that some anticipated earlier adopters are actually later adopters, or some identified later adopters are actually earlier adopters. Teachers, after gaining additional knowledge, may have increased or decreased interest in the change. Leaders may also discover early signs of possible resistance.

Contrary to natural urges, leaders need to maintain their efforts with earlier adopters and later adopters before dealing with resisters. Leaders need to build a critical mass of support for the change. Frequently, once a high majority of teachers have adopted the change and are using it successfully, resistance dissipates.

What follows is another possible scenario, this one involving the use of the theory behind levels of adoption among adults confronted with a change initiative and employing the tool we've provided to identify early adopters and counter rejection.

SCENARIO 2: REACHING THE EARLIER ADOPTERS

A high school principal and district mathematics coordinator are in a state that has recently agreed to adopt the CCSS. Both the principal and coordinator have remained informed about the CCSS and knew they would face significant changes at the high school level in mathematics. They believed the content would pose a few problems but nothing too extreme. Every mathematics teacher at the high school was certified and very capable of teaching the mathematical content. The serious problems would arise with changes in instructional strategies and building toward student success in higher-level mathematics courses.

The mathematics coordinator felt she needed to start working with the teachers on changing their instructional approaches, even though previous efforts had not proved overly effective. The principal, however, believed she had a plan and wanted the coordinator's ideas and support. The principal believed that, if she could get her teachers to routinely administer and score common, open-ended assessments, her teachers would gradually change their practices.

Each six weeks, students were given benchmark assessments. These assessments were district wide and district scored. The problems on the assessments were all multiple choice. The data were returned in a timely manner, but the principal and coordinator knew it currently had little impact on instruction. The principal decided she wanted her teachers to also give an open-ended assessment every six weeks but between the six-week benchmarks.

Her four-point plan was the following:

1. Have teachers administer and score an open-ended assessment.

2. Have teachers begin collaborating on creating the open-ended assessment.

3. Standardize through a rubric scoring of the open-ended assessment.

4. Have teachers develop, administer, grade, and collaboratively analyze the common assessment.

She intended to start with her Algebra I and Geometry teachers. To help her and the coordinator get started, she decided to use the Levels of Adoption form (Figure 3.1). She provided a copy of the form to the coordinator. They discussed the form and then independently placed the names of the teachers in the three quadrants—initiators, earlier adopters, and later adopters. They agreed to record their individual thoughts and then meet the next day.

The following day, the principal and coordinator met to discuss the form. They compared their responses and generally agreed. In the few cases where they disagreed, they further discussed the placement and then mutually agreed in which quadrant to place the teachers. For the next several days, the principal and coordinator located various articles on common assessments and printed the CCSS mathematical practices. The principal and coordinator next held a meeting with the teachers they considered to be earlier adopters. During the meeting, the principal explained her plan, provided materials, and asked the members to think things over during the next several days. She asked her teachers to get back with her concerning their interest and questions.

The following week, the principal held a meeting with her Algebra I and Geometry teachers. The coordinator was present, but the principal conducted the meeting. She explained her plan with the goal of administering and scoring common assessments. She provided the articles to the teachers and then involved everyone in a conversation about the mathematical practices. She pointedly asked for teachers to think about and discuss the relationship between common assessments and the mathematical practices. She explained that she was forming a leadership team to assist with the plan and introduced the teachers who had expressed interest.

The leadership team met with the coordinator to create common assessments. The teachers administered the assessments and then met to discuss the results. They supported the idea but felt there was much more to learn. The principal called another meeting with the Algebra I and Geometry teachers.

The principal encouraged all her teachers to include more open-ended problems in their tests but mandated that all teachers administer a single six-week open-ended assessment and to score student work rather than just the answer. The principal asked her teachers to think about her plan outline and offer any changes or suggestions. She encouraged them to talk to the leadership team and coordinator.

Because the benchmark was to be administered in two weeks, the mandated open-ended assessment would take place in five weeks. She ended the meeting by stating that she, the coordinator, and leadership team members would be meeting with the teachers independently or in small groups over the next several weeks.

Over the next few weeks, meetings were held with the teachers. Following the meetings, the coordinator, principal, and leadership team revisited their Levels of Adoption form and affirmed who they believed were the initiators, earlier adopters, and later adopters. The principal honed in on the earlier adopters and asked for their specific input, concerns, or issues. She directly asked for their help and support. Further, she directly asked them if they believed this change was important if the CCSS mathematical practices were to be attained in their classrooms.

As the time approached for the open-ended assessment, the coordinator met with the initiators and asked for help in writing one open-ended item for Algebra I and one item for Geometry. Once these items were written, the coordinator asked the earlier adopters to review the problems and make changes if necessary. The items, with minor changes, were approved, copied, and distributed.

Following the administration and grading of the items, the coordinator took random samples from all classrooms and made copies of the papers. The range of student answers, quality of work, and grading was vast. The principal and coordinator met with the leadership team to review the students' work. In this meeting, the coordinator and principal mostly remained silent as the leadership team expressed real concerns about the obvious differences in student work and understanding of mathematics.

The leadership team asked for principal and coordinator assistance in meeting with the Algebra I and Geometry teachers so the differences could be shared and discussed. They also requested that the open-ended assessments be given every three weeks. The principal was confident that the following discussions would lead to consistency in grading and acceptable standards of student work.

As the principal's plan unfolded, she, the coordinator, and interested team members monitored classrooms for evidence of changing instructional strategies. They continued to record which teachers were making progress and which teachers needed additional support. The initiators and earlier adopters clearly understood that students needed to be more engaged in classroom activities with more opportunities to work and discuss open-ended, more challenging problems. The mathematics coordinator was busier than ever as he coplanned and cotaught lessons with the teachers.

With the administration of each open-ended assessment, the level and quality of student work improved across the courses. Grading became more consistent, and teacher collaboration greatly increased.

Reflection

In this scenario, the groups move forward as positive pressure is applied. Monitoring is supportive and encouraging and shows progress and improvement. As adoption is fostered, rejection and resistance are diminished. As teachers gain proficiency in the change, leaders observe a shift from engagement to empowerment.

Naturally, this is a vision for how the adoption process can best be implemented, and as such, it is optimistic—but we do not feel it is unrealistic. We have seen this process work well in the districts where we consult.

Next, we turn to our second strategy—focusing on student success—which must be infused throughout the change process; it is, after all, the point of any change and the motivating factor for teachers and administrators alike.

QUESTIONS FOR DISCUSSION

Is rejection a serious problem?

How is rejection manifested or not manifested in your school?

In Scenario 1, The Unadopted Plan, or Scenario 2, Reaching the Earlier Adopters, what was occurring from the principal's point of view?

In the same scenarios, what was occurring from the teachers' points of view?

What do the Levels of Use of the Innovation mean for change?

How can the Levels of Adoption form (Figure 3.1) be effectively used and inappropriately misused?

4 Focusing on Students Brings Success

With any change initiative, student success and achievement in mathematics are the primary intents. Previous efforts may have been generally unsuccessful. This lack of success, as we have stated, is most often due to a failure to adequately build the necessary foundations, including collaborative efforts. While student success is the desired outcome, preplanning and foundation work is critical if leaders do not want to repeat prior mistakes. The work demands understanding between leaders and teachers concerning instructional classroom expectations and behaviors. This chapter highlights important mutual understandings leaders and teachers need to have that are related to student success. Mutual understandings serve to support effective leadership teams and study groups.

Both leaders and teachers will face many challenges in adopting and implementing the CCSS for mathematics. Some of these challenges can be easily anticipated, such as matching and aligning content, replacing inappropriate materials, transitioning students to new content standards, and shifting classroom instructional strategies. Knowing that these challenges are staring leaders in their faces does not really make the challenges any easier to deal with. Yet fear truly resides with the unknown. If readers can anticipate and plan for these known challenges and the known challenges alone push at the maximum resource limit, what happens when something unanticipated but critical emerges from the shadows?

In anticipating the known challenges and recognizing there will be unknown challenges, we provide five big ideas concerning student learning and achievement. These ideas do not operate independently but intersect. While logistical problems may emerge, such as printing and distributing materials and organizing meetings, most conceivable challenges for instruction can be clustered beneath one of these five big ideas. Familiarity with these ideas provides leaders and teachers ways to handle surprises. If student achievement based on collected data related to the CCSS mathematics content and student practices indicates learning difficulties, one or more of the big ideas is most likely the culprit.

BIG IDEA 1: THE OPPORTUNITY TO LEARN

One of the most straightforward and easiest to understand of the big ideas is opportunity to learn. Students absolutely must be taught the appropriate mathematical content for the grade or course in which they are enrolled. While the CCSS in mathematics certainly help move toward clarity, there are still content decisions to be made, such as depth, sequence, arrangement, and support materials. The better delineated the documents are, the easier it is to provide opportunity to learn. If the correct content is not being taught or even taught inadequately, then assessment data generated by benchmark tests, teacher-made tests, published tests, and state assessment tests are completely inaccurate because they do not correctly assess what was actually taught.

When opportunity to learn correct content is missing, leaders— unaware of the problem—assume data are reflective of students' abilities or perhaps indicate the poor quality of the instructional materials. As a result, they may actually make unnecessary or unproductive changes to curriculum documents or materials. For sure, they are faced with providing extra assistance to students who would not need extra assistance had they been exposed to the correct content. This extra assistance dilutes the time and effort for truly needy students.

Two very important ideas emerge in relation to opportunity for students to learn the identified, specified content. Marzano (2003) suggests that leaders provide a "guaranteed" and "viable" curriculum. A viable curriculum is one that can actually be taught within the designated time frame of the grade level or course. As curriculum documents are created or adapted, leaders ensure that the length of time recommended in the documents reasonably matches the time allotted for instruction. Curriculum documents include a scope, sequence, timeline, and materials.

A guaranteed curriculum is one that leaders and teachers are positive is being taught to every student. Once curriculum documents are created and approved, leaders monitor their use in classrooms. If the foundational curriculum documents are flawed, opportunity to learn is denied.

Lurking in the Shadows

In identifying and dealing with unknown challenges, leadership teams should ensure that the opportunity to learn is not responsible for the lack of success or poor results. As data are generated, weaknesses will appear. Leadership teams need to make sure old ideas and materials are not still in use in classrooms.

BIG IDEA 2: VISIBLE THINKING

Visible thinking means that students and teachers are aware of their thought processes when organizing and solving problems (Hull, Balka, & Harbin Miles, 2011b). Being cognizant of how you think and what you are thinking is a life skill. In order to learn mathematics with meaning, students must connect the new content to their current understanding. This is possible only if students are aware of their current knowledge level. Our presentations often start with a premise: Thinking is a requirement for learning mathematics. No one has ever disputed this premise, yet student thinking is often unintentionally devalued in mathematics classrooms. Teachers must make thinking intentional.

To develop an understanding about thinking, students first need to solve problems that require some degree of thinking, such as the two problem examples that follow—one at the elementary or middle level and one at the secondary level. Many times in mathematics classrooms, thinking is actually overlooked as students and teachers focus on honing procedural skills. Fluency with procedural skills is important, but it is also only a small part of learning mathematics. Focusing on procedural skills in mathematics is like focusing on learning spelling words by rote and assuming it will improve reading comprehension. In the same vein, students do need to read fluently, but what benefit is it to students who can pronounce fluently but have no comprehension of the material they just covered?

Example One (Grades 4–6): Divisibility Using Number Tiles

Domain: 4-OA—Operations and Algebraic Thinking

Standard: Gain familiarity with factors and multiples.

Cluster 4: Find all factor pairs for a whole number in the range 1–100. Recognize that a whole number is a multiple of each of its factors. Determine whether a given whole number in the range 1–100 is a multiple of a given one-digit number. Determine whether a given whole number in the range 1–100 is prime or composite.

Domain: 6-NS—The Number System

Standard: Compute fluently with multi-digit numbers, and find common factors and multiples.

Cluster: 2: Fluently divide multi-digit numbers using the standard algorithm.

As students in the middle grades begin preparing for their study of algebra, knowledge of various divisibility tests helps them in many ways, particularly in factoring. The CCSS, however, do not offer a specific cluster where the tests are a focus. The emphasis is placed on the idea of factors of a number.

Basic tests for divisibility are generally limited to particular factors. A number is:

- Divisible by 2 if the ones digit is even (0, 2, 4, 6, 8).
- Divisible by 3 if the sum of the digits in the number is divisible by 3.
- Divisible by 4 if the last two-digit number is divisible by 4.
- Divisible by 5 if the ones digit is 0 or 5.
- Divisible by 6 if the number is divisible by 2 and by 3.
- Divisible by 8 if the last three-digit number is divisible by 8.
- Divisible by 9 if the sum of the digits is divisible by 9.

Typically, practice problems using the tests are limited, such as the following:

Which of these numbers has a factor of 9?

A. 39   B. 369*   C. 1069   D. 4349

One divisibility test is used, and not much student thinking is evident.

Consider instead the use of 0 to 9 number tiles, either commercially made clear plastic tiles or card-stock cutouts.

Provide students with several numbers with missing digits and indicating factors for divisibility of the numbers. Students must consider various tests for each number before correctly arranging the tiles.

For example:

Use any eight number tiles 0 through 9 to create four 3-digit numbers, each divisible by the given factors.

		Answer
Divisible by 2 and 9	☐ 8 ☐	(882)
Divisible by 2 and 5	☐ 4 ☐	(440)
Divisible by 4 and 9	5 ☐ ☐	(576)
Divisible by 3 and 5	4 ☐ ☐	(495)

In creating the three-digit numbers, students must consider all of the divisibility tests (2, 3, 4, 5, and 9) as they attempt to find an overall solution to the problem. Although certain digits satisfy particular divisibility tests on one number, using them often creates unsolvable situations for other numbers. With more than one correct answer, the problem lends itself to class discussion, which is an important part of making student thinking visible.

Two (Grades 8-10): Quadratic Equations

Domain: A-REI—Reasoning with Equations and Inequalities

Standard: Understand solving as a process of reasoning and explain the reasoning.

Cluster 4b: Solve quadratic equations by inspection (e.g., for $x^2 = 49$), taking square roots, completing the square, the quadratic formula, and factoring as appropriate to the initial form of the equation. Recognize when the quadratic formula gives complex solutions, and write them as $a \pm bi$ for real numbers a and b.

Consider the use of the quadratic formula in Algebra 1 or Algebra 2. Students typically learn it as a procedural skill without understanding the intricacies. That is:

$$\text{If } ax^2 + bx + c = 0, \text{ then } x = \frac{-b \pm \sqrt{b^2 - 4ac}}{2a}$$

Given a quadratic equation, they procedurally substitute values into the formula to find the two solutions to the equation, and they are done. However, if they are given only parts of each, they often lack the thinking necessary to comprehend what is missing.

For example:

Arrange the digits 0–9 in the squares so that every quadratic equation is correct.

If $x^2 - 5x - \square = 0$, then $x = \dfrac{5 \pm \sqrt{\square\square}}{2}$

If $x^2 + 4x - \square = 0$, then $x = \dfrac{-\square \pm \sqrt{52}}{2}$

If $x^2 - \square x + 4 = 0$, then $x = \dfrac{6 \pm \sqrt{2\square}}{2}$

If $x^2 + \square x - 3 = 0$, then $x = \dfrac{-3 \pm \sqrt{\square\square}}{2}$

In solving the problems, students must think about both the quadratic equation and the quadratic formula as they go back and forth to place the digits. Thinking and understanding are required to comprehend where to place the digits.

Visible thinking in mathematics involves comprehension. When students read and study problems, they understand words and symbols. They can translate words into mathematical statements with appropriate symbols, and they can translate mathematical statements involving symbols into words. Both teachers and students need to hear what the students comprehend and how they are translating. As students hear themselves, they develop their voices and vocabularies for explaining their thinking. Eventually, students develop an inner dialogue or inner voice that operates as they work through problems of various degrees of challenge.

The idea of visible thinking must be instituted in mathematics classrooms. Students need to hear teachers explain not just how to work a problem but how teachers organized their thoughts, drew upon their knowledge, opted for a solution path, learned from this path what worked and what did not, and then tried another path until they were successful. Persistence in solving problems is not developed if the first path selected is always the correct path or the only path students know.

Lurking in the Shadows

Success in mathematics teaching and learning requires students to actively think, discuss, and share. When data identify difficulties in certain areas of mathematics, leaders need to ensure that rote learning is not the dominant approach to instruction. Also, leaders need to validate that the classroom climate is conducive to thinking and sharing ideas. Finally, leaders need to ensure that appropriate materials are being used. Material design heavily influences instructional strategy selection and usage.

BIG IDEA 3: ENGAGING LESSONS

Engaging lessons work with visible thinking. Engaging lessons are mathematics lessons that students cannot "sit out." Far too often in mathematics classrooms, students are allowed to voluntarily disengage from classroom activities. In such classrooms, there are often two tacit expectations: Do not sleep, and do not disrupt. If students are called upon to give an answer, they may freely admit that they do not know, or they can provide some wild guess. In either situation, the teacher often moves on to another student.

One strategy for engaging students in a lesson titled "Pass the Question—A Writing Strategy" is offered by Anderson and Brown (2011):

> Purpose: This strategy provides students with the opportunity to construct and write their thoughts regarding a specific topic. Additionally, students have the chance to evaluate another student's work and revise or elaborate on that response as needed.
>
> Procedures: Students are given a prompt and asked to write a short response. Students trade responses. Students review the response they have been given and then revise the response (add, subtract, or correct information in the response). Students can then be allowed time to discuss with each other why the responses were revised.

For example, students are asked to draw upon their previous lessons regarding equations of straight lines. Here are possible prompts:

1. Two straight lines intersect when:

2. Two lines are parallel when:

3. Two lines are the same line when:

To be engaging, tasks must be interesting and challenging for students to want to invest time and energy. Engaging lessons also include cooperative grouping so students can share ideas with partners. Students know they are held accountable for the mathematical knowledge. To not know the answer to a question or problem is not a difficulty, but to not know the answer by the end of class is simply not allowed.

Lurking in the Shadows

Student engagement and active participation work together. When data emerge that indicate trouble spots in achievement, leaders need to ensure that engaging lessons are occurring. Sometimes, lessons may appear engaging when they are not. If individual students are providing single-word answers to teacher-directed questions for a majority of the class time, then only surface-level engagement is happening. In other situations, teachers may work through challenging problems with the entire class rather than allow small groups of students to work on the task.

BIG IDEA 4: GROUP-WORTHY PROBLEMS

To meet the demands of the eight Standards for Mathematical Practice, students will need to work challenging problems—problems that do not have a single solution path or even one "right" answer. These types of problems also challenge teachers. Teachers are very aware of the problem degree of difficulty dilemma. If the problem is too easy, students are disinterested and bored. If the problem is too difficult, students are overwhelmed and frustrated. Collaborative groups and group-worthy problems balance degree of difficulty, address appropriate learning objectives, and focus on student practice. According to Lotan (2003, pp. 72–75) group-worthy problems have five design features:

- They are open-ended and require complex problem solving.
- They provide students with multiple entry points to the task and multiple opportunities to show intellectual competence.
- They deal with discipline-based, intellectually important content.
- They require positive interdependence as well as individual accountability.
- They include clear criteria for the evaluation of each group's product.

These five features support teachers in addressing, and students in learning, mathematics with meaning. They also provide opportunities for addressing the correct content, visible thinking, engaging lessons, and timely intervention.

Lurking in the Shadows

Group-worthy tasks are challenging problems that require the thinking of more than one student and frequently three or four students. If group-worthy tasks are not occurring in classrooms at an expected degree of frequency, then leaders need to carefully check instructional materials. The difficulty likely resides in instructional materials that are not conducive to discussion and collaborative work. Leaders may need to collaborate with teachers to construct appropriate tasks for various grade levels or courses.

BIG IDEA 5: TIER 1 RESPONSE TO INTERVENTION AND ONGOING FORMATIVE ASSESSMENT

Opportunity to learn, visible thinking, engaging problems, and group-worthy problems provide classroom situations where students actively think about the mathematical content they are supposed to be thinking about. Earlier, we discussed that students should not be allowed to disengage from learning. Appropriate intervention is a direct result of visible thinking, and visible thinking emerges from challenging, engaging, and group-worthy problems.

Timely intervention is another way of referring to ongoing formative assessment. Feedback provided through ongoing formative assessment in classrooms has a tremendous positive effect on student learning and understanding. For this reason, and the fact that intervention is often misunderstood, this section is given significant space.

Intervention is a much-needed skill for classroom teachers and required knowledge for leaders. The Response to Intervention (RTI) system that is currently being used in the United States is a three-tier system that offers various levels of support. Commonly held descriptions of the levels are presented in Table 4.1.

Table 4.1 Response to Intervention System

Tier 1	Primary Intervention	High-quality core instruction that meets the needs of most students
Tier 2	Secondary Intervention	Evidence-based intervention(s) of moderate intensity that addresses the learning or behavioral challenges of most at-risk students
Tier 3	Tertiary Intervention	Individualized intervention(s) of increased intensity for students who show minimal response to secondary intervention

One of the most important things to understand for both teachers and leaders is that immediate, effective interventions in the classroom solve the need for more intrusive and disruptive Tier 2 and Tier 3 interventions.

Missed Opportunities

With the shift to the CCSS mathematics content, and especially to the mathematical practices, students will need effective intervention strategies. Due to sheer numbers of students likely needing assistance with increased expectations, teachers will have to handle many of the interventions within their classrooms. If students are being constantly shuttled in and out of the mathematics classroom, they will just fall further behind.

When discussions emerge and focus on RTI, educators' misunderstandings abound. The confusion seems to stem from the use of the word *intervention*. Interventions are thought to relate to actions teachers take after some type of formal assessment occurs. While this is accurate in one sense, it truly is a limited view, understanding, and approach. Intervention of this type will quickly overwhelm teachers and support staff.

Effective intervention should occur during multiple levels of the teaching–learning cycle. To truly be effective, intervention needs to occur during planning, presenting, analyzing, and reflecting—the phases of the teaching improvement cycle identified by Hull, Harbin Miles, and Balka (2010).

Planning for Intervention

Including intervention during planning may at first seem counterintuitive or illogical. This is a significant mistake in judgment. Effective lesson planning is far more involved than merely identifying the content to be taught. Teachers need to plan for what content is taught, how the content is taught, and how the students will demonstrate their understanding of the content (assessment). Teachers should clearly identify assessment approaches before the lesson is ever taught. Building lessons around how students will demonstrate their understanding is the vehicle teachers use to intervene and correct misunderstandings. Planning is the time for teachers to recall common student misconceptions or errors and to ensure that classroom activities are designed to alleviate or greatly reduce these common mistakes. Planning is also the time to carefully consider strategies as well as the eight student practices.

Presenting for Intervention

During lesson presentation, teachers are guiding students through the planned lesson activities. Engaging activities with opportunities for students to explore and discuss allow teachers a chance to utilize ongoing formative assessment strategies. These strategies (such as pair-share and every student response) allow students a chance to make their thinking visible to their teachers, classmates, and themselves (National Research Council, 2000). With information gained from these strategies, teachers are able to immediately respond to and correct students' errors and misunderstandings. The sooner misunderstandings are confronted and addressed, the easier they are to remediate. Mistakes, once learned, are far more difficult to correct.

Analyzing for Intervention

Educators frequently confuse lesson analysis and reflection. Effective reflection is based upon careful lesson analysis. Lesson analysis directly relates to student-demonstrated learning and therefore relates to intervention.

Lesson analysis is an unbiased, unemotional recording of the lesson events. Analysis can be thought of as a videotape or lesson script. Analysis is the time to capture exactly what occurred in the classroom during the lesson presentation. Analysis answers questions such as the following:

- What did the teacher say?
- What did the students say?
- What did the teacher do?
- What did the students do?
- What evidence was collected concerning student performance?
- How did the students perform on the assessment?

Once the sequence and events are captured, then analysis is used to answer two additional questions:

- What parts of the lesson were presented as planned?
- What parts of the lesson deviated from the plan?

Lesson analysis does not attempt to answer the question of *why*. Why things happened is preserved for reflection.

Reflecting for Intervention

Once lesson analysis has been completed, lesson reflection can be initiated. Reflection puts emotion and opinion back into the improvement process. Reflective questions may ask the following:

- What parts of the lesson went well?
- What parts of the lesson did not work well?
- Why were (or were not) changes made in the lesson?

- Where did students seem to understand the content?
- Where did students seem to not understand the content?
- What strategies or approaches may have worked better?
- What needs to be done concerning student weaknesses?

These questions demand honesty if lesson quality and teaching are to improve. As lessons gain in quality and strength, less need for extensive intervention is the result.

Intervention Strategies

Finally, reflective practice feeds directly into the planning process. As future lessons are planned, teachers need to carefully consider to what degree intervention strategies are needed. For instance, teachers may consider the following ideas:

- Scaffold in future lessons
- Problem of the day
- Small instructional group reteach
- Whole-class reteach

Scaffold in future lessons. Teachers may be able to provide appropriate intervention by scaffolding skills or concepts in future lessons. Scaffolding requires teachers to review and explain prerequisite skills or concepts just before they are needed in the new lessons.

Problem of the day. Teachers may be able to strengthen skills or concepts through regular, brief practice during the first few minutes of class.

Small instructional group reteach. Teachers need an adequate supply of challenging and worthwhile games. Games serve as excellent and highly motivational ways to have students practice skills and improve concept connections. With games, teachers are able to have students independently work in small groups. This provides teachers time to directly reteach selected students.

Whole-class reteach. Occasionally, teachers find it necessary to intervene with the entire class of students. As a note, frequent instances of whole-class reteach are a "red flag" that strongly indicates a mismatch between student learning approaches and lesson instructional strategies. Whole-class reteach should consist only of totally redeveloped and restructured lessons. Repeating the lesson that did not work is an incredible waste of valuable instructional time.

Teachers, support staff, and leaders need to work to improve their understanding of intervention. The two strategies—ongoing formative assessment and intervention—work hand in hand. Effective teachers routinely check for student understanding, and when misunderstandings are detected, immediate corrections occur.

Lurking in the Shadows

When data are indicating that too many students are being unsuccessful, leaders need to ensure that proper intervention is occurring. Three problems emerge with intervention. First, intervention is not immediate. Effective intervention is ongoing during classroom instruction. Second, intervention is not appropriate. Effective intervention targets the specific mathematics problem the student is having. Third, intervention is based on beliefs. Some teachers do not believe their job is to offer extra assistance.

Intervention Example

The following area and perimeter problem is used in the CCSS to demonstrate how a traditional approach to teaching a concept that students frequently struggle to understand can be transformed into a conceptual approach. The transformed problem approach allows teachers multiple opportunities to appropriately intervene with students and correct errors in thinking.

Students often struggle with the measurements of area and perimeter. In many cases, these geometric concepts are taught at the same time and in

---

Example Problem: Area and Perimeter

Domain: 3—Measurement and Data

Standard: Recognize area as an attribute of plane figures and understand concepts of area measurement.

Cluster 5a: A square with a side length of 1 unit is called *a unit square*, is said to have *one square unit* of area, and can be used to measure area.

Cluster 5b: A plane figure, which can be covered without gaps or overlaps by *n* unit squares, is said to have an area of *n* square units.

Cluster 8: Solve real-world and mathematical problems involving perimeters of polygons, including finding the perimeter given the side lengths, finding an unknown side length, and exhibiting rectangles with the same perimeter and different areas or with the same area and different perimeters.

Source: CCSS (2010).

isolation. In the traditional instructional approach shown in the box below, students often do not have to look beyond the visual cues. They do need to recall whether the answer is in inches or square inches. With this level of instruction, it is little wonder students fail to remember area and perimeter.

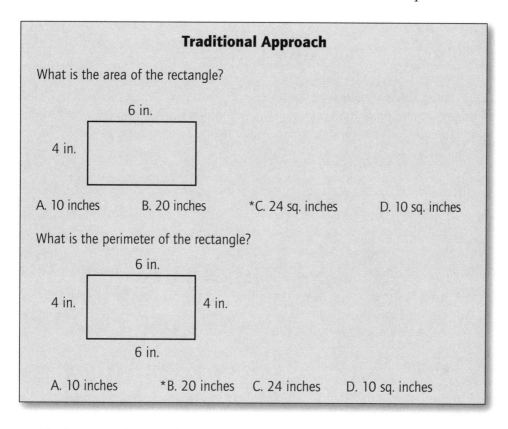

Traditional Approach

What is the area of the rectangle?

6 in.

4 in.

A. 10 inches   B. 20 inches   *C. 24 sq. inches   D. 10 sq. inches

What is the perimeter of the rectangle?

6 in.

4 in.   4 in.

6 in.

A. 10 inches   *B. 20 inches   C. 24 inches   D. 10 sq. inches

Eschewing this traditional approach, the CCSS example instead encourages students to learn area as a way to provide meaningful multi-plication facts. Multiplication can be represented as rectangular arrays, in the alternative problem approach that follows.

Transformed Problem Approach for Student Pairs

Part 1: A rectangle has a perimeter of 32 feet. In whole numbers, what are the possible dimensions of the rectangle?
    Using 32 unit tiles, students construct various rectangles with a perimeter of 32 feet and record the measurements such as the following:

1 + 15 + 1 + 15
2 + 14 + 2 + 14

(Continued)

(Continued)

Part 2: After the students have found various sizes and compared answers with others from the classroom, student pairs write the rectangular dimensions.

1 × 15	4 × 12	7 × 9
2 × 14	5 × 11	8 × 8
3 × 13	6 × 10	

Part 3: Student pairs then create an organized table.

Length	Width	Perimeter	Area
15	1	32	
14	2	32	
•	•	•	
•	•	•	
•	•	•	
8	8	32	

When the table is completed, students discuss the patterns.

Part 4: Students re-create with unit tiles several shapes randomly selected by the teacher from the table.

The following script suggests what a teacher may say during instruction:

We constructed a rectangle with perimeter of 32 units and side measures of 12 + 4 + 12 + 4.

Look at one of the tiles. What shape is the tile? (Square)

For one tile, what is the length of one side? (1)

If the length of each side is one, what is the perimeter of the tile? (4)

The tile is made in the shape of a square. The perimeter is the distance around the outside edges of the square, but what is the measurement of the interior or center part of the square? (Class discussion of ideas)

Count the number of tiles used to create the rectangle that is 14 by 2. (28)

We counted square tiles; so let's say the measurement is 28 square tiles.

Construct a rectangle that is 10 by 6, and then count the number of tiles. (60)

Let's say the measurement is 60 square tiles.

Why isn't the measurement staying the same like the perimeter did?

(Class discussion)

Mathematicians named this inside or interior measurement *area*, and the measurement is in square units.

Construct one more rectangle of 15 by 1. What is the area? (15 square units)

Return to the table, and fill in the area for each rectangle.

What are the dimensions of the rectangle that has the greatest area? What do you notice about this particular rectangle?

What is happening to the dimensions (length and width) in relation to the area?

SCENARIO 1: THE TEXTBOOK

A school district, needing to change mathematics instruction, decided to hire a mathematics coordinator. The coordinator was excited about the job possibility and certainly wanted to do a good job. After accepting the position, the coordinator decided to study the school district data.

The first thing the coordinator discovered was that fourth grade and fifth grade tests scores on the district annual assessments had been very low in mathematics for many years. The trend was not repeated in third grade or sixth grade. The coordinator was definitely puzzled. She decided to look into the state content standards for these grades. She found that, at the state level, fractions were emphasized in fifth grade and decimals were emphasized in fourth grade.

According to the district curriculum documents, this was exactly the same emphasis. The coordinator was puzzled but quickly became distracted by the many requirements of the newly created job. The issue did not arise again until the end-of-the-year assessment results were completed. Again, fourth grade and fifth grade scores were lower than any of the other grades.

The coordinator was still perplexed but believed she had better get to the bottom of this problem. Her focus next year was going to be on these two grades. As the year started, the coordinator did indeed pay more attention to Grades 4 and 5. She monitored the scope and sequence and visited classrooms when fractions or decimals were presented.

She went to the nearest elementary school and stopped in to watch a fourth grade lesson, as she had done numerous times. Only this time, she was intentional about watching the decimal lesson unfold. She was stunned to discover that decimals were not taught during the lesson, but fractions were. The teacher had opened her textbook, informed the students of the page, and taught a complete lesson regarding adding fractions with like denominators.

The coordinator left the room, returned immediately to her office, and rechecked the scope and sequence as well as the state content. Most definitely, recognizing decimals to the 100ths place was supposed to be the lesson. Because the scope and sequence recommended several days of instruction on this topic, the coordinator went out the next day to check as many fourth and fifth grade classrooms as possible. As she now expected, fifth grade teachers were teaching decimals, and fourth grade teachers were teaching fractions in spite of the scope and sequence and district documents.

The adopted textbook series offered a concentrated focus on decimals in fifth grade and fractions in fourth grade, just the opposite of the state content and district emphasis. As a result, teachers were teaching from the book when it came to these topics. This was a significant problem because appropriate materials were not available for fractions in fifth grade or decimals in fourth grade. The coordinator immediately began working with the fourth and fifth grade teachers to shift to the correct content.

SUMMARY: FOCUSING ON STUDENTS FOR SUCCESS

Students are the reason we have schools. Given a chance to redesign schools, not many of today's students would re-create our current system. In the early grades, students are excited about coming to school and learning. Sadly, this excitement usually ends before third grade. This clearly should not be the case. Students should not be praying for bad weather days or just "holding on" until the holidays. Our society reflects this attitude when the news media discuss how "happy" students are that they do not have to go to school on a particular day.

With the advent of the CCSS, we have an opportunity to fundamentally change classroom instruction, at least in mathematics. The Standards for Mathematical Practice are not drudgery or more memorization but indicators of excitement, engagement, purpose, and productivity. Every school administrator, when walking into classrooms, should first look at the students. Are they happy, excited, involved, talking, sharing, discussing, debating, analyzing, and most of all, doing mathematics?

If these events are not occurring, the eight identified mathematical practices are also not occurring. Leaders responsible for mathematics can easily recognize these classroom attributes by watching students for just a brief moment of time.

QUESTIONS FOR DISCUSSION

Why is the opportunity to learn important for teachers and students?

How can the theme *visible thinking* help promote coherence and collaboration?

What is the potential impact on student achievement from ongoing formative assessment and RTI?

In Scenario 1: The Textbook, misalignment is obvious. What misalignment can be a concern in your school or on your campus?

5 Attaining the Common Core Practices

A t this point in our book, leaders and teachers have addressed two strategies that support change like that indicated in the CCSS and student practices. Leaders have created leadership teams that work to (1) promote adoption by avoiding rejection as well as to (2) maintain a focus on student success. In Chapter 5, leaders, teachers, and teams specifically work to move forward in adopting required changes specific to the Standards for Mathematical Practice.

In Chapter 3, readers were provided with a Levels of Adoption form (Figure 3.1) for assistance in working with teacher groups as they manage change. The form helps leaders reflect on their teachers, and organize initiators, earlier adopters, later adopters, and perhaps resisters. The job for leaders and leadership teams is to build support for change initiatives by bringing more teachers on board according to their preference for dealing with change.

In this chapter and Chapter 6, leadership teams are provided resources to help in their task of moving more teachers toward adopting the Standards for Mathematical Practice.

UNDERSTANDING THE STANDARDS FOR MATHEMATICAL PRACTICE

The Standards for Mathematical Practice, as delineated and explained in the CCSS, are based on previous research and reasoning from the NCTM (2000) in the *Principles and Standards for School Mathematics* and from the

NRC (2001) in the book *Adding It Up.* These identified CCSS practices and supporting research provide the conditions under which students learn mathematics with deep conceptual understanding. From this foundation, the mathematics development teams of the CCSS created a list of eight standards of student practice that push leaders and teachers to think carefully about how students learn mathematics as well as how they demonstrate learning proficiency. Figure 5.1 demonstrates the relationship among NCTM standards, NRC proficiencies, and the CCSS practices.

Figure 5.1 Comparison of Standards: CCSS, NCTM, and NRC

CCSS	NCTM	NRC
1. Make sense of problems and persevere in solving them	Problem solving	Productive disposition
2. Reason abstractly and quantitatively	Reasoning and proof	Procedural fluency
3. Construct viable arguments and critique the reasoning of others	Communication Reasoning and proof	
4. Model with mathematics	Representation	Conceptual understanding
5. Use appropriate tools strategically	Problem solving	Strategic competence
6. Attend to precision	Connections	
7. Look for and make use of structure	Connections	Adaptive reasoning
8. Look for and express regularity in repeated reasoning	Reasoning and proof	Adaptive reasoning

These eight practices and supporting research are challenging to understand in regard to what they mean for students and teachers. Even more challenging, once some mutual understanding is reached, is how these phrases translate into student and teacher actions.

For example, selecting one of the practices such as number 2 (reason abstractly and quantitatively with CCSS, reasoning and proof with NCTM, and procedural fluency with NRC), we are immediately confronted by a host of questions: What do classrooms look like that are addressing these practices? What are teachers doing, and how are students responding? And perhaps the most critical question is this: What instructional strategies support this practice and supporting phrases, and which ones do not? These same questions must be asked and answered for the remaining seven practices. This task is far too complex to be answered by individual teachers or mathematics leaders. It requires a team effort.

These questions lead to one more significant question: Are the strategies currently being used in mathematics classrooms sufficient to have students demonstrate proficiency on the Standards for Mathematical Practice? The answer to this last question is a resounding no!

Deciding on appropriate instructional strategies presents all leaders and teachers with very real dilemmas. If teachers must include additional strategies, how are they to decide which strategies to include? Are some strategies more effective than others? How much teacher instructional change is reasonable within a given time frame? What is the role of leadership in supporting these changes? Assistance in addressing these dilemmas is provided in the proficiency matrix, strategy sequence chart, and sample problems that follow.

UNDERSTANDING INDICATORS OF PROGRESS

After reading the practices delineated in the CCSS, it is apparent to us that the mathematical practices are not skill-based content that students can learn only through direct teaching methods but rather ones that emerge over time from opportunities and experiences provided in mathematics classrooms. These opportunities and experiences must include challenging problems, student collaborative groups, interactive discourse, and adequate time—clearly not easy tasks.

Complementary forms that identify degrees of proficiencies for the practices (Figure 5.2) and a strategy sequence (Figure 5.3) are offered to assist teachers, leaders, and leadership teams in successfully and progressively transitioning classroom instructional strategies to meet the expectations contained in the eight Standards for Mathematical Practice. Leaders and team members should already be familiar with these documents. If not, leadership teams should now acquaint themselves with the forms. Copies of these two documents are needed when working through the sections below. They can be found not only in this chapter but also at the end of the book as foldout pages that are perforated for convenience.

Common Vocabulary

In discussing and working with our two forms, teachers and leaders may find it useful to share a common vocabulary that we have developed

Figure 5.2   Understanding the Proficiency Matrix

Standards of Student Practice in Mathematics Proficiency Matrix

	Students:	(I) = Initial	(IN) = Intermediate	(A) = Advanced
1a	**Make sense of problems.**	Explain their thought processes in solving a problem one way. *(Pair-Share)*	Explain their thought processes in solving a problem and representing it in several ways. *(Questioning/Wait Time)*	Discuss, explain, and demonstrate solving a problem with multiple representations and in multiple ways. *(Grouping/Engaging)*
1b	**Persevere in solving them.**	Stay with a challenging problem for more than one attempt. *(Questioning/Wait Time)*	Try several approaches in finding a solution, and only seek hints if stuck. *(Grouping/Engaging)*	Struggle with various attempts over time, and learn from previous solution attempts. *(Allowing Struggle)*
2	**Reason abstractly and quantitatively.**	Reason with models or pictorial representations to solve problems. *(Grouping/Engaging)*	Translate situations into symbols for solving problems. *(Grouping/Engaging)*	Convert situations into symbols to appropriately solve problems as well as convert symbols into meaningful situations. *(Encouraging Reasoning)*
3a	**Construct viable arguments.**	Explain their thinking for the solution they found. *(Showing Thinking)*	Explain their own thinking and thinking of others with accurate vocabulary. *(Questioning/Wait Time)*	Justify and explain, with accurate language and vocabulary, why their solution is correct. *(Grouping/Engaging)*
3b	**Critique the reasoning of others.**	Understand and discuss other ideas and approaches. *(Pair-Share)*	Explain other students' solutions and identify strengths and weaknesses of the solutions. *(Questioning/Wait Time)*	Compare and contrast various solution strategies, and explain the reasoning of others. *(Grouping/Engaging)*

	Students:	(I) = Initial	(IN) = Intermediate	(A) = Advanced
4	**Model with mathematics.**	Use models to represent and solve a problem, and translate the solution into mathematical symbols. *(Grouping/Engaging)*	Use models and symbols to represent and solve a problem, and accurately explain the solution representation. *(Question/Prompt)*	Use a variety of models, symbolic representations, and technology tools to demonstrate a solution to a problem. *(Showing Thinking)*
5	**Use appropriate tools strategically.**	Use the appropriate tool to find a solution. *(Grouping/Engaging)*	Select from a variety of tools the ones that can be used to solve a problem, and explain their reasoning for the selection. *(Grouping/Engaging)*	Combine various tools, including technology, explore, and solve a problem as well as justify their tool selection and problem solution. *(Allowing Struggle)*
6	**Attend to precision.**	Communicate their reasoning and solution to others. *(Showing Thinking)*	Incorporate appropriate vocabulary and symbols in communicating their reasoning and solution to others. *(Allowing Struggle)*	Use appropriate symbols, vocabulary, and labeling to effectively communicate and exchange ideas. *(Encouraging Reasoning)*
7	**Look for and make use of structure.**	Look for structure within mathematics to help them solve problems efficiently (such as 2 × 7 × 5 has the same value as 2 × 5 × 7, so instead of multiplying 14 × 5, which is [2 × 7] × 5, the student can mentally calculate 10 × 7). *(Question/Prompt)*	Compose and decompose number situations and relationships through observed patterns in order to simplify solutions. *(Allowing Struggle)*	See complex and complicated mathematical expressions as component parts. *(Encouraging Reasoning)*
8	**Look for and express regularity in repeated reasoning.**	Look for obvious patterns, and use if/ then reasoning strategies for obvious patterns. *(Grouping/Engaging)*	Find and explain subtle patterns. *(Allowing Struggle)*	Discover deep, underlying relationships (uncover a model or equation that unifies the various aspects of a problem such as discovering an underlying function). *(Encouraging Reasoning)*

Source: LCM: mathleadership.com. Reprinted with permission.

Figure 5.3 Understanding the Strategy Chart

Instructional Implementation Sequence: Attaining the CCSS Mathematical Practices Engagement Strategies

Strategy	Description	Practice	Degree	Matrix Code
Initiating think-pair-share	Pair-share, or think-pair-share, is a strategy easy to implement in any classroom at any grade level or subject. This strategy does not require any other change in pedagogy or materials. For pair-share, teachers merely ask a question or assign a problem and allow students to think and work with a partner for one to three minutes before requesting an answer to the question or problem. In think-pair-share, students are given a brief period of time to think independently before working with a partner. While effective in results, this strategy is a significant first step in engaging all students in classroom instructional activities.	Make sense of problems.	Explain their thought processes in solving a problem one way.	**1a I**
		Critique the reasoning of others.	Understand and discuss other ideas and approaches.	**3b I**
Showing thinking in classrooms	Teachers need to work toward higher degrees of student involvement in classroom activities. Once pair-share is incorporated into classroom routines, teachers need to incorporate additional strategies that promote Every Pupil Response (EPR). EPR strategies include such responses as thumbs-up/thumbs-down, or use of individual whiteboards for noting answers. Students are also pressed to be more aware of their thinking and express their thinking in more detail.	Construct viable arguments.	Explain their thinking for the solution they found.	**3a I**
		Model with mathematics.	Use a variety of models, symbolic representations, and technology tools to demonstrate a solution to a problem.	**4 A**
	Students are routinely asked to share their thinking in mathematics classrooms. However, what is routinely accepted as thinking is actually procedural description. Students merely provide the steps they used to solve the problem, not their reasoning and thinking about how they knew which processes to use. In order to reveal student thinking, more challenging, open-ended problems are needed.	Attend to precision.	Communicate their reasoning and solution to others.	**6 I**

Strategy	Description	Practice	Degree	Matrix Code
Questioning and wait time	As thinking is increased in mathematics classrooms, better questioning and wait time are required. Teachers need to provide thought-provoking questions to students, then allow the students time to think and work toward an answer.	Make sense of problems.	Explain their thought processes in solving a problem and representing it in several ways.	**1a IN**
		Persevere in solving them.	Stay with a challenging problem for more than one attempt.	**1b I**
		Construct viable arguments.	Explain their own thinking and thinking of others with accurate vocabulary.	**3a IN**
		Critique the reasoning of others.	Explain other students' solutions and identify strengths and weaknesses of the solutions.	**3b IN**
Empowerment Strategies				
Grouping and engaging problems	The strategy of grouping and engaging problems is a significant shift in pedagogy and materials. Students are given challenging problems to work and allowed to work on the problem in a group of two, three, or four. Challenging mathematics problems take time, effort, reasoning, and thinking to solve.	Make sense of problems.	Discuss, explain, and demonstrate solving a problem with multiple representations and in multiple ways.	**1a A**
		Persevere in solving them.	Try several approaches in finding a solution, and only seek hints if stuck.	**1b IN**
		Reason abstractly and quantitatively.	Reason with models or pictorial representations to solve problems.	**2 I**

(Continued)

(Continued)

Strategy	Description	Practice	Degree	Matrix Code
		Reason abstractly and quantitatively.	Translate situations into symbols for solving problems.	**2 IN**
		Construct viable arguments.	Justify and explain, with accurate language and vocabulary, why their solution is correct.	**3a A**
		Critique the reasoning of others.	Compare and contrast various solution strategies, and explain the reasoning of others.	**3b A**
		Model with mathematics.	Use models to represent and solve a problem, and translate the solution into mathematical symbols.	**4 I**
		Use appropriate tools strategically.	Use the appropriate tool to find a solution.	**5 I**
		Use appropriate tools strategically.	Select from a variety of tools the ones that can be used to solve a problem, and explain their reasoning for the selection.	**5 IN**
		Look for and express regularity in repeated reasoning.	Look for obvious patterns, and use if/then reasoning strategies for obvious patterns.	**8 I**

Strategy	Description	Practice	Degree	Matrix Code
Using questions and prompts with groups	Once students are provided with opportunities to solve challenging problems in groups, teachers need to increase their ability to ask supporting questions that encourage students to continue working, provide hints or cues without giving students the answers, and ask probing questions to better assess student thinking and current understanding.	Model with mathematics.	Use models and symbols to represent and solve a problem, and accurately explain the solution representation.	**4 IN**
		Look for and make use of structure.	Look for structure within mathematics to help them solve problems efficiently.	**7 I**
Allowing students to struggle	Students learn to persevere in solving challenging mathematics problems by being allowed to struggle with challenging problems. Students need to understand that mathematical problems do not usually have quick, easy solutions. Effective effort is a life skill and should be learned interdependently and independently. Appropriate degree of difficulty is foremost on teachers' minds. If the problem is too easy, students do not need to struggle. If the problem is far too difficult, students are not capable of solving the problem. Teachers need to balance working in groups and working independently and be able to quickly adjust grouping strategies as the need arises.	Persevere in solving them.	Struggle with various attempts over time, and learn from previous solution attempts.	**1b A**
		Use appropriate tools strategically.	Combine various tools, including technology, explore, and solve a problem as well as justify their tool selection and problem solution.	**5 A**
		Attend to precision.	Incorporate appropriate vocabulary and symbols in communicating their reasoning and solution to others.	**6 IN**
		Look for and make use of structure.	Compose and decompose number situations and relationships through observed patterns in order to simplify solutions.	**7 IN**

(Continued)

(Continued)

Strategy	Description	Practice	Degree	Matrix Code
		Look for and express regularity in repeated reasoning.	Find and explain subtle patterns.	8 IN
Encouraging reasoning	Students need to be encouraged to carefully think about mathematics and to understand their level of knowledge. They also need to be able to accurately communicate their thinking. Reasoning, in this context, is used to convey having students stretch their understanding and knowledge to solve challenging problems. Reasoning requires students to pull together patterns, connections, and understandings about the rules of mathematics and then apply their insight to finding a solution to a difficult, challenging problem.	Reason abstractly and quantitatively.	Convert situations into symbols to appropriately solve problems as well as convert symbols into meaningful situations.	2 A
		Attend to precision.	Use appropriate symbols, vocabulary, and labeling to effectively communicate and exchange ideas.	6 A
		Look for and make use of structure.	See complex and complicated mathematical expressions as component parts.	7 A
		Look for and express regularity in repeated reasoning.	Discover deep, underlying relationships (uncover a model or equation that unifies the various aspects of a problem such as discovering an underlying function).	8 A

Source: From *Visible Thinking in the K–8 Mathematics Classroom*, by T. H. Hull, D. S. Balka, and R. Harbin Miles, 2011, Thousand Oaks, CA: Corwin. Copyright by Corwin. Reprinted with permission.

to explain the working relationship between the horizontal documents. The definitions of these terms as we use them are as follows:

- Proficiency Matrix: Short abbreviation for Standards of *Student Practice in Mathematics Proficiency Matrix.*
- Sequence Chart: Short abbreviation for *Instructional Implementation Sequence: Attaining the CCSS Mathematical Practices Engagement Strategies.*
- Practice: The eight identified Standards for Mathematical Practice from the CCSS.
- Proficiency: Attaining mastery of the standards through the phases of (I)nitial, (IN)termediate, and (A)dvanced.
- Indicator: Description of student actions that depict the degree of mastery of the selected practice.
- Strategy: One of the instructional approaches from our list of seven sequential instructional techniques.
- Cell: One of the numerous boxes created by the intersection of the horizontal and vertical descriptors from either of our documents.

Students' abilities develop as opportunities are provided. With teacher guidance, students' abilities build across indicators of proficiency. In our matrix, *Standards of Student Practice and Mathematics Proficiency Matrix*, we designate the degrees of proficiency as (I)nitial, (IN)termediate, and (A)dvanced and offer indicators of proficiency for each practice. To help students continue in a pattern of growth with mathematical proficiency, our matrix is offered to teachers and leaders as a way to consider and gauge students' progress for each of the practices as the students demonstrate proficiency for each indicator.

The eight student practices are interdependent and do not develop in isolation from one another. While it is possible, and probably desirable, to focus on a few practices within a lesson unit, all mathematics educators need to continually assess student progress on these practices in a holistic fashion. Furthermore, in using the matrix, mathematics teachers and leaders need to apply their knowledge of grade-appropriate content and pedagogy to adjust our indicators of progress.

When looking at the Proficiency Matrix, leaders and teachers will observe the left-hand column of numbers from 1 to 8 for the eight practices, with practices 1 and 3 having a and b parts. We felt in these particular instances that the mathematical practices had dual components that were significant enough to merit individual proficiency scales.

For instance, by looking at practice number 2 (reason abstractly and quantitatively) within Figure 5.2, readers observe three cells that move left to right along the row, with each cell indicating a greater degree of proficiency.

Practice 2 (from the Proficiency Matrix)

Practice	Students:	(I) = Initial	(IN) = Intermediate	(A) = Advanced
2	Reason abstractly and quantitatively.	Reason with models or pictorial representations to solve problems. *(Grouping/ Engaging)*	Translate situations into symbols for solving problems. *(Grouping/ Engaging)*	Convert situations into symbols to appropriately solve problems as well as convert symbols into meaningful situations. *(Encourage Reasoning)*

Source: LCM: mathleadership.com. Reprinted with permission.

The degree (I, IN, A) is determined by moving horizontally across the Proficiency Matrix cells from left to right. Within each cell for this particular practice are descriptions of what we would expect students to be doing. The other seven practices follow this same format.

In the Proficiency Matrix, readers will also see a shortened description of strategies included in each cell. These descriptions directly relate to instructional strategies identified in our second form: *Instructional Implementation Sequence: Attaining the CCSS Mathematical Practices Engagement Strategies* (Figure 5.3).

The Proficiency Matrix (Figure 5.2) works in parallel to our companion document *Instructional Implementation Sequence: Attaining the CCSS Mathematical Practices Engagement Strategies* (Figure 5.3). The sequence of instructional strategies is from Hull, Balka, and Harbin Miles (2011b, p. 86) and provides teachers with a progressive, developmental approach toward incorporating new instructional strategies. As strategies are incorporated and mastered, the Standards for Mathematical Practice are attained, student achievement increases, and student learning is greatly enhanced.

The sequence is:

1: Initiating think-pair-share (or pair-share)

2: Showing thinking in classrooms

3: Questioning and wait time

4: Grouping and engaging problems

5: Using questions and prompts with groups

6: Allowing students to struggle

7: Encouraging reasoning

In using the sequence system for this book, we have combined it with the information represented in the Proficiency Matrix by having each indicator of proficiency listed below the instructional strategy in the Sequence Chart. For instance, if readers look at Figure 5.3, they notice that our first recommended strategy is *think-pair-share* and is identified as pair-share in the matrix cells. The pair-share strategy, when implemented by teachers, focuses on indicator 1a I (explain their thought processes in solving a problem one way or, in other words, the Initial Level of Practice 1a) and indicator 3b I (understand and discuss other ideas and approaches or the Initial Level of Practice 3b). As a result, when teachers work to incorporate each successive strategy, they are also achieving proficiency of the student practices.

In working with this implementation sequence, mathematics teachers and leaders must remember that the strategies are cumulative. Each prior strategy supports the next one. Strategies are not used and then forgotten. The strategies are enhanced and expanded with each successive strategy. Additionally, with the cumulative nature of these strategies, there is also a major shift in pedagogy and belief. This shift is described as moving from engagement to empowerment. Both teachers and students need time to adjust to higher degrees of proficiency. First, teachers and students must become engaged in the strategy sequence and initial degrees of proficiency. Over time, with teachers moving at different rates, both teachers and students gain empowerment.

Leadership teams can assist in making the shift by providing all mathematics teachers with these two resources and then involving teachers in conversations that support their moving from engagement to empowerment strategies. Steady progress is highly recommended. Teachers add strategies at different rates, so it is not unreasonable to work only on engagement strategies in the first year.

Readers find that our sequence lists seven strategies. Leaders, leadership teams, and teachers understand there are certainly variations of the strategies that can be effectively utilized to achieve the same results, such as questioning and wait time. Teachers can ask many open-ended questions in classrooms of students that engage and encourage all students to think before providing answers. There are also additional research-based strategies teachers can effectively use in their classrooms. Many of these strategies can be inserted into either or both forms if desired. Our purpose was not to provide an overwhelming number of strategies or an exhaustive list but, rather, to provide a reasonable, manageable, sequential way for teachers to implement instructional change in their classrooms and directly improve student mathematical learning and achievement.

The cross-reference nature of the two forms assists teachers in planning effective lessons that encourage participation, learning, and variety of strategy usage and that target specific student practices. The recommendations contained in Chapter 4, Focusing on Students Brings Success, all support the ideas identified in the Proficiency Matrix and Sequence Chart.

Understanding and incorporating significantly different instructional strategies are often daunting for many teachers and leaders. Our desire is to provide tools based on the mathematical practices identified in the CCSS that assist mathematics leaders and teachers in the improvement processes of planning, presenting, analyzing, and reflecting (Hull, Balka, & Harbin Miles, 2009) in a manageable sequence. By following the recommended processes outlined in our forms, students' progress in achieving the Standards for Mathematical Practice can be assessed and success in mathematical learning attained.

WORKING WITH THE PROFICIENCY MATRIX AND SEQUENCE CHART

These two forms assist leadership teams and teachers during the improvement process of collaborative lesson planning, lesson presenting, team analyzing of the lesson, and team reflecting on the lesson. The forms are cross-referenced, so information is easy to locate on the chart or matrix. Collaborative planning and reflecting encourages and supports change.

Lesson Planning

In planning lessons, teacher teams need the Sequence Chart and Proficiency Matrix available, plus any local or state curriculum documents. Collaborative planning steps include the following:

1. Teacher teams identify content to be taught in a lesson (one or more days).

2. Teams consider what mathematics students are to know and how students could best demonstrate understanding.

3. Teams carefully consider the strategies needed to help students learn the content.

4. Teams select instructional strategies they have mastered or think need to be used.

(What are the instructional activities teachers intend to use? For instance, they may have been working on the strategy sequence and have incorporated pair-share, think-pair-share, and showing thinking in class.)

5. Teams turn to the chart and locate the cells identified with pair-share and showing thinking.

(The matrix cells are 1a I [make sense of problems: explain their thought processes in solving a problem one way], 3a I [construct viable arguments: explain their thinking for the solution they found], 3b I [critique the reasoning of others: understand and discuss other ideas and approaches], 4 A [model with mathematics: use a variety of models, symbolic representations, and technology tools to demonstrate a solution to a problem], and 6 I [attend to precision: communicate their reasoning and solution to others]).
With this information, the teams know that students need to:

- (1a I) explain their thought processes in solving a problem one way
- (3a I) explain their thinking for the solution they found
- (3b I) understand and discuss other ideas and approaches
- (4 A) use a variety of models, symbolic representations, and technology tools to demonstrate a solution to a problem
- (6 I) communicate their reasoning and solution to others

Teachers realize that not every one of the four indicators needs to be used in the next lesson, but they clearly know students need time to discuss their solutions and think with other students as well as with teachers. As a result, teachers plan several opportunities for students to work with partners.

6. Teams formulate several questions they can pose to the class to get students thinking and explaining their thinking. Teams consider student prior knowledge and experience as well as the connectivity of the content to future lessons.

7. Teams consider possible responses from students and common errors students make.

8. Teams sequence content flow and activities and identify strategies for the activities.

9. Teams clarify, define, and develop assessment activities.

Lesson Presenting

In presenting, teachers want to ensure that they provide adequate time for students to discuss in pairs. As much as possible, they want to follow the collaboratively planned lesson. However, teachers are also alert to the need of adjusting if student confusion arises.

Team Analyzing of the Lesson

Lesson analyzing is a process of capturing what happened in the classroom as the lesson unfolded. Analysis does not include opinion of what worked or what did not but rather what happened as planned and what changes were made. Following the lesson presentation, teachers make notes about the presented lesson.

At the next team meeting, teacher teams reread the indicator they wanted the students to experience during the lesson. In this particular example, they wanted students discussing their thinking and comparing their solutions.

During the analysis process, teacher teams discuss the individual notes concerning the flow of the lesson. For instance, teachers may have generally noted that students were engaged when working with partners and readily shared their thought processes for solving the problem. Teachers also noted that most pairs gave equal time to partners. They did have to take time to remind students of some previous content. With only minor adjustments, the teams determine that the lesson followed their plan.

Team Reflecting on the Lesson

Team reflection follows the analysis process. Reflection places professional opinions back into the process. Reflection uses observations and student work to determine lesson effectiveness and suggest possible recommendations for improvement or refinement. If changes were made to the lesson, explanations for the change are provided and discussed.

As an example, the teacher teams were generally pleased with the lesson. They did feel the students needed to work more at expressing their thought processes rather than their procedures. They decided to have each student independently record how the pair solved the problem in the next lesson. In this way, teachers could pull some examples of good thinking to show students. Teams also thought they needed to model solving a problem where teachers articulated thinking. Finally, teams made notes in their planning book to be sure to review the prerequisite skills just before allowing the students to work in pairs.

DEGREES OF PROFICIENCIES AND STRATEGIES EXAMPLES

Instructional strategies used by teachers directly impact the degree of mathematical proficiency students obtain. By studying and understanding the relationship between the mathematical practices Proficiency Matrix and the instructional strategy Sequence Chart, teachers, teacher teams, leadership teams, and leaders recognize the developmental nature of student engagement and learning with meaning. Combining this knowledge with sample problems presents leaders and leadership teams with the link between strategy selection and use and classroom materials.

The Standards for Mathematical Practice will not be achieved without instructional change—change that directly increases student involvement and engagement in the mathematics classroom. Student engagement does not increase without challenging problems. Students will need to be taught how to collaborate, to persevere, and to become aware of their thinking. In order to emphasize this point, and to help visualize the team's use of the Proficiency Matrix and Sequence Chart, we provide multiple problems at different grade levels in the appendix at the back of this book.

Each sample problem included in the appendix focuses on certain strategies and degrees of proficiency. As encouraged in the discussion of planning, presenting, analyzing, and reflecting, teacher collaborative teams are highly recommended. Team collaboration is a skill developed over time after teachers have experienced many opportunities to work together. Frequently, teacher collaborative teams need a discussion point at which to start. For this reason, multiple sample problems are provided. The easy-to-use strategy of think-pair-share is very uncomplicated but tremendously enriching. We offer numerous examples of this strategy.

Finally, teachers and leaders must not assume the strategies and practices are a one-way continuum. Lessons flow up and down the Proficiency Matrix and practices as well as back and forth. Lessons have various intents and purposes related to the content. Teachers select the appropriate strategies (once all have been learned) and the appropriate degree of proficiency (based upon maturity level and desired degree of mastery).

SCENARIO 1: THE THIRD-YEAR TEACHER

A third-year third grade teacher has been working to include mathematics content from the CCSS into her classroom. She has had minimal support and advice, as most of the other third grade teachers have not made any effort to shift strategies or content. She has a copy of the CCSS for her grade level and attempts to locate appropriate ones for her school assigned scope and sequence.

The teacher has decent classroom control, but it is clearly not as strong as that of many of the other teachers in her school. Yet she deeply feels her students are just not learning mathematics, and she is truly concerned. Earlier in the year, she found an open-ended, grade-appropriate problem that she felt her students would enjoy. She knew students would need to be problem solvers and thinkers when the CCSS assessments started arriving, and she wanted to be prepared.

On a Friday, the students spent part of the class period reviewing material from the week and reciting their math facts. She decided to stop the review early and challenge her students with the new problem. She handed out copies of the problem to her students and told them she wanted them to see if they could solve it and to record their thinking in the space below the problem. She further added that they would really enjoy working on this kind of problem.

The problem had barely reached the last student before hands began going up.

"What are we supposed to do? There aren't answers."

"I don't understand."

"Are we supposed to know this?"

The teacher asked the students to put their hands down. She told the students that this problem was designed to help them think and that they just needed to read the problem and think about it. In a few minutes, hands began going back up.

"Is this a test?"

"Will you help me?"

"I don't know where to start."

One of the teacher's brighter students in the front of the room was beginning to quietly cry. Other students just put their heads down on their desks. She told the class to get out their library books and spend time silently reading. She would come around and collect the papers.

Now, she is uncomfortable in her position of wanting to get her students more engaged and excited while still keeping control. To date, control has won out. When she thinks about trying something new, memories flood back about the "problem day." She is just relieved she didn't get any parent calls.

At the next faculty meeting, the teachers were informed that a mathematics specialist had been hired to help the district move forward on teaching content from the CCSS. On the first day of her visit, the specialist met with each teacher.

The specialist asked the teachers to talk about the students in their classes and how the students were doing in mathematics. She also informed teachers that she would be visiting each and every classroom over the next few weeks.

When the third-year teacher met with the specialist, she was unusually quiet. She truly did not know what to say. She tried to answer about her class, but she knew she was vague. In the next few days, the specialist came to her classroom during her planning period. The third-year teacher was greatly concerned.

The specialist stated that she knew the teacher wanted to tell her something, and the specialist understood how difficult it was to confide in a stranger. The specialist stated that anything the teacher told her would be in strict confidence. The specialist was here to help the students, and if the choice came between sharing their private conversation and leaving her consulting contract, she would leave her contract. The specialist asked if she could come back sometime during the week to either visit her classroom or visit during the planning period. The third-year teacher asked the specialist to please visit her mathematics class on Thursday.

On Thursday, the specialist arrived right on time. She asked the teacher if she could help her by working with students who had questions. The teacher agreed and began her lesson. The specialist constantly was on the move helping various students as the teacher explained the lesson, worked examples, and then gave an assignment. At the end of the class period, the specialist told the teacher that she truly appreciated the opportunity to visit her class and work with her students. Later in the day, the teacher found a note in her box from the specialist. Again, she thanked her for allowing her to work with her students and added, "It is obvious to me that you care a great deal for your students. Let me know if you would like to visit or have me return."

The third-year teacher made an appointment during her planning period with the specialist as soon as possible. The specialist had barely entered the room when the teacher asked, "So, how do you think my lesson went?" The specialist said, "We can certainly talk about that if you like, but first, why don't you tell me about your students?"

The third-year teacher barely took a breath as she told the specialist about her students, her concerns, her "problem day," her isolation, and her deep concern that she was cheating the students out of good mathematics.

The specialist told the teacher that her students were returning to class. She asked the teacher for a copy of the problem and said that she would return the following day and they could plan a lesson together. The teacher agreed. The next day, the specialist arrived on time. She explained to the teacher about think-pair-share. Together, they worked out a plan whereby the teacher would explain the strategy to the students and then use the strategy two times during the first half of the lesson. Then, the specialist would take over the class as they tackled the problem.

The class was a huge success. The problem was solved in student pairs, and students could barely wait to explain what they had done. The class ran 15 minutes over the scheduled time. The teacher and the specialist began a professional working relationship that lasted for years.

SUMMARY: ATTAINING THE COMMON CORE PRACTICES

Leaders now possess several pieces of very important information concerning how adults adopt change and how students develop proficiency in the eight practices. With these tools teachers can use a sequence of instructional strategies to gradually transition their classrooms from the current status to one more engaging and better aligned with utilizing the mathematical practices for assessing students' mathematical knowledge and understanding.

CONTINUING PROGRESS

As a sequence of strategies is implemented, teacher teams, leadership teams, and leaders will discover students moving into higher degrees of proficiency on the practices. This process is gradual and maintained at a steady pace. If strategy implementation is rushed, teachers have not had time to perfect the strategy, and students have not had time to reap the benefits of the strategy. If strategy implementation is too slow, the strategy becomes stale and less effective. Even though they are ready, students are not being challenged to higher degrees of proficiency in the practices.

With this level of understanding, it is time to enter a hypothetical classroom. This journey inside a classroom draws information from previous chapters and provides a concrete model for discussion.

QUESTIONS FOR DISCUSSION

What needs to be done to promote adoption of new strategies that support the CCSS mathematical practices?

How will students immediately benefit from the new strategies?

How can you use the Sequence Chart to support planning for change?

How can you use the Proficiency Matrix to support change efforts?

6 Visiting a Transforming Classroom

This chapter provides readers with an example of a mathematics lesson that is planned, presented, and analyzed. Teacher teams and leadership teams are expected to critique lesson components and provide reflection. To accomplish this, readers step inside Mr. Young's fourth grade mathematics lesson, as well as "see" Mr. Young's thoughts. At the end of each day, Mr. Young briefly reflects on the classroom events in preparation for needed instructional shifts. At the end of five days, Mr. Young reflects on the unit in planning for the next instructional unit.

By using this "visit" as a learning tool for shared conversations, leadership and teacher teams are free to openly discuss Mr. Young. The "visit" provides a neutral source of classroom information without having to use teachers from the school or district as examples. Readers note that Mr. Young is not presented as working in a team because some schools face constraints concerning collaborative teaming. The scenario is easily adapted to collaborative planning if the reader so desires.

Mr. Young is not offered as a role model or exemplar for change actions. An optimal pace is not the same for every teacher. If readers recall the discussions concerning overcoming resistance, then they recall that teachers tend to move in groups. For this reason, monitoring is critical. Leaders and teams need to carefully read Chapter 8, Maintaining Support to Increase Implementation, in order to ensure an appropriate instructional pace. Leaders and leadership teams are not to use Mr. Young as a benchmark.

BACKGROUND

Mr. Young is a sixth-year teacher in an elementary school of about 700 students. He greatly enjoys teaching and working with students. Mr. Young believes in interactive classrooms, but he essentially remained a very traditional teacher for his first four years. Mr. Young did begin using games in his classroom, but he was unsure of how to appropriately use other engaging instructional strategies. Two years ago, Mr. Young attended a training session that frequently used the strategy think-pair-share, and he felt he could use this strategy with his students.

Mr. Young's state adopted the CCSS and is working toward implementation over the next several years. He was provided a copy of the CCSS fourth grade content and descriptive matter that explained the mathematical practices. Mr. Young's principal has asked the teachers to study the CCSS content and make efforts to include it when appropriate. The district is working on updating and refining all of its curriculum documents.

Mr. Young is intrigued by the mathematical practices but is unsure about how some of them actually look in a classroom. While he has a good professional working relationship with other teachers, his principal, and the district mathematics coordinator, there is not actually any person he feels he can talk to about these practices.

During his last after-school staff meeting, the district mathematics coordinator attended. The mathematics coordinator handed out two documents to the teachers. The coordinator had found these documents online and believed they could help teachers incorporate instructional strategies that focused on the practices as well as support their work in helping students demonstrate proficiency on the practices. These documents were *Instructional Implementation Sequence: Attaining the CCSS Mathematical Practices Engagement Strategies* and *Standards of Student Practice in Mathematics Proficiency Matrix*. Mr. Young began using these documents as a way to plan his mathematics lessons and then analyze and reflect on them. He also asked the mathematics coordinator to work with him on clarifying his understanding of the documents. At this time, Mr. Young was working on place value for multi-digit numbers. The related standard is shown below.

COMMON CORE STANDARDS GRADE 4: NUMBER AND OPERATIONS IN BASE TEN

Generalize place value understanding for multi-digit whole numbers.

1. Recognize that, in a multi-digit whole number, a digit in one place represents 10 times what it represents in the place to its right.

2. Read and write multi-digit whole numbers using base-ten numerals, number names, and expanded form. Compare two multi-digit numbers based on meanings of the digits in each place using >, =, and < symbols to record the results of comparisons.

3. Use place value understanding to round multi-digit whole numbers to any place.

PLANNING THE LESSONS

Mr. Young is very familiar with his district's curriculum documents as well as the content standards he is to teach. He felt his challenge was to add appropriate depth from the CCSS. For the next week, Mr. Young intends to work with his students on place value to 10,000. He also wants his students to compare two numbers and use the phrases *greater than* and *less than*. After studying the CCSS, he decided to include rounding and to remind his students of the symbols for *greater than* and *less than*. After reading over the mathematical practices, Mr. Young felt he needed to include an application for rounding and decided to increase his students' knowledge of estimating.

Mr. Young decided to start with numbers to 100. He wanted his students to mentally calculate two addends that summed to 100. He believed in having mathematics make sense to students, and he wanted his students to use reasoning when solving problems. He had taught rounding in the past as a skill and was dissatisfied that students were unable to use rounding as a way to check the reasonableness of their answers.

Mr. Young believed that, as students found the missing addend to 100, the students would develop a better feel for numbers. He could use this idea to launch a discussion about relative size of the missing addend and estimating a reasonable answer. He then could work with students to actually perform rounding in the context of approximating an answer to an addition problem. He could use the same ideas when he worked with subtraction.

After rounding, he thought he could return to place value to have students compare two numbers and then select the appropriate symbols to show the relationship. Finally, he wanted to pull everything together into an activity that he could use to assess student understanding.

Once Mr. Young had this flow developed, he began creating his daily lessons. He studied both documents he had received from the mathematics coordinator. Mr. Young believed he was on the third strategy (questioning and wait time) and beginning the fourth strategy (grouping and engaging problems). As a result, he knew he wanted to constantly use pair-share, wait time, entire class response, and ongoing opportunities for assessment of students' understanding. He also wanted to include some larger group activities with open-ended type responses, so he could truly check for student thinking and understanding.

Mr. Young studied the Proficiency Matrix to ensure he was having his students steadily making progress. For this week's series of lessons, he was focusing on having his students reason abstractly and quantitatively, construct viable arguments, and critique the reasoning of others with some work in looking for and making use of structure.

PRESENTING

Day 1 Lesson: Compose and Decompose Numbers to 100

Setting the Stage

Mr. Young: Class, today we want to study number combinations to 100. You know that 10 is a benchmark number that can help you mentally add and subtract. One hundred is also a benchmark number. Let's review combinations of 10. If I said 6, what would you answer for the number needed to reach 10? (4) What if I said 3? (7)

As a reminder, we have used several strategies in the past to help us with these combinations, such as a number line, counting down, and counting on. Today, we want to expand our ability to reach the benchmark of 100. The same strategies work, but they also become too time-consuming to use for every situation. If I gave you the number 80, you could count down from 100. Let's do that: 100, 90, 80, and I have counted down two 10s or 20. So, 80 plus 20 is 100. Let's take 70 and use counting up. That's 70, 80, 90, 100, and I have counted up three 10s, so 70 plus 30 equals 100. We could also think about what I could add to 7 to make 10 and then multiply by 10 to get our answer: 3 multiplied by 10 is 30.

Now, I want you to think about this next problem by yourself. What would you do if I gave you 25? (Wait time)

Tell your neighbor what you did to solve this and what your answer is. Now, let's share some strategies:

Student 1: I added 5 to 25 and got 30. Then, I counted up to 100 by 10s and got 7 tens. Now, 70 plus 5 is 75, so 25 plus 75 equals 100.

Mr. Young: Did anyone else do this?

Would another student like to explain? What other way did you solve this?

Student 2: I know 25 plus 75 is 100, so I used what I knew to get 75.

Mr. Young: Who else did this? (Hands raised) Another way? (Calling on another student)

Student 3: I added 25 to 25 to get 50 and then added 50 plus 25 to get 75.

Mr. Young: I don't quite understand. How did you get to 100?

(At this time, the principal stepped into the classroom on his walk-through visit looking for student engagement. The lesson continued uninterrupted.)

Student 3: I had 25, so I added another 25 to get 50. I need 50 more to get to 100, so I added the 50 and 25 to get 75. Then, 75 plus 25 is 100.

Mr. Young: Thank you. I get it now. I see one particular answer emerging. Did everyone get 75, or is there another answer? (No response) Did every neighbor pair agree? (Yes)

OK, let's take a bit more challenging problem. This time, work with your neighbor to get an answer. What if I gave you 83?

(After wait time, students discuss various ways such as 80 + 20 = 100, so 20 − 3 is 17. 83 + 17 = 100. Then, 83 plus 7 more is 90 plus 10 is 100.)

Exploring

Mr. Young: Students, I want you to get with your partners. Each pair will have a spinner (0 to 9), a place value mat (100s, 10s, 1s), and base ten blocks of 1s and 10s. (Linking cubes can be used, with 9 sets of 10 linked together and 9 single cubes.)

Students, take turns spinning the spinner. The first digit goes in the 10s column, and the second spin digit goes in the 1s column.

100	10	1

The student who spins first selects the correct number of base ten blocks needed for the 1s column, and the second student places the 10s blocks in the 10s column. Both students then record the two addends and the answer of 100. Let's work one together. (Pointing to a student) Would you come spin for the 10s column?

(The student spins a 3, and Mr. Young places three 10s in the 10s column. Another student comes up and spins a 7 for the 1s place. Mr. Young places seven 1s in the 1s column.)

100	10	1

Mr. Young: I have 37. (Mr. Young calls on a student to fill in the 1s, and the student puts three in the 1s column.) I'm going to fill in the 10s, and I want you to check what I do. Let's see—three 10s plus seven 10s makes 100 (Mr. Young puts seven 10s blocks in the 10s column.) So, 37 plus 73 equals 100.

Students, talk with your partner, and check my work. Did any group get a different answer? Several hands go up. (Mr. Young calls on one group and asks if there is a problem with his work. The students say that he forgot about the 10.) Can you tell me more? I don't understand. (One of the students says that, when he added 7 and 3, he got 10 and forgot to move it to the 10s column.) Can you come show me? (The student comes to the front and says that 3 plus 7 is 10, so you have to move a 10 over to the 10s column and leave zero in the 1s column.)

Mr. Young: Talk with your partner about what John just said. Do you agree or disagree?

(After discussion, and Mr. Young feels everyone understands, he does one more problem that he spins, and the partners work and write down the addend, addend, and sum. After observing, he instructs the students to play five games.

Summarizing

Mr. Young: Students, when you were playing the benchmark game, what strategies did you use to find the missing addend? (Students talk about using facts they know, adding on, subtracting, etc.)

Now, I want you to think about this before I call on someone to answer. Look at your sheet of recorded answers. When you were finding the missing addend, how would you know if the second addend would be greater than 50, less than 50, or equal to 50? You're homework is to bring your written answer to class tomorrow.

Daily Analysis

For the most part, the lesson unfolded as planned. From observing their work, Mr. Young knew the students were able to find the missing addend. He had run out of time at the end of the lesson.

Daily Reflection

Mr. Young was glad he added the lesson section about regrouping the 1s column. He had forgotten to plan that part but remembered the trouble it had caused last year. He had it in his lessons now. The homework assignment was an afterthought and probably a complete waste of time because he did not take time to clearly set his expectations.

Day 2 Lesson: Rounding

Setting the Stage

Mr. Young: Yesterday, we worked on finding combinations of two addends that summed to exactly 100. Get back with your partner, and play five more rounds of the game. Only this time, I want you to do the calculations mentally. Here is what I want you to do and then write down. You will spin for the 10s digit like this—I got a 2. Spin for the 1s digit, and I got an 8. So, one addend is 28. What is the second addend? I think to myself that 8 plus 2 is 10, so I record the 2 in the 1s place. Then, I think 2 plus 8 is 10, but I have to remove one

10 because I regrouped, so I only need seven 10s. I write down the 7 in the 10s place. Now, I have 28 plus 72 equals 100. Notice I only wrote down the first addend, the second addend, plus sign, equals sign, and 100: 28 + 72 = 100.

(Students play five rounds of the game while the teacher moves about the room observing and listening.)

Mr. Young: OK, class, as I was moving around, I noticed that Brenda and Sarah had 56 as their first addend. I knew their second addend was going to be less than 50. I noticed that Sam and Linda had a first addend of 34, and I knew their second addend would be greater than 50.

How did I know this?

Share your homework response with your partner, and discuss what you think is the answer to my question. (Students work in pairs.)

Mr. Young: Who has an answer to share? Yes, Amanda, what are you thinking?

Amanda: I looked at the number in the 10s place. If it was 5 or higher, I knew the next addend would be less than 50. If the number in the 10s place was less than 5, then I knew the next addend would be greater than 50. I didn't get an exact 50, so I didn't think about it.

Mr. Young: Amanda, that is very good thinking. So, if the digit in the 10s place was a 5, 6, 7, 8, or 9, then you knew the next addend would be less than 50. If the digit in the 10s place was a 0, 1, 2, 3, or 4, then you knew the next addend would be greater than 50. What to you think would happen if you did spin 50?

Amanda: They would be tied.

Mr. Young: What do you mean by tied?

Amanda: Both addends are 50.

Mr. Young: Good work, Amanda. Class, do we have a symbol we could use to show that 50 and 50 are equal?

(Students respond with "equal sign," and teacher writes 50 = 50.)

Mr. Young: Class, I want to explain to you a skill in mathematics we can use to help estimate answers. This skill is named *rounding,* and it uses the information you just discovered about combinations summing to 100. Remember, we discussed estimating answers. Estimation is a mathematical understanding that allows someone to quickly arrive at an approximate answer without being exact, yet the answer is appropriate to the situation.

Rounding can be used at times to help you estimate an answer. Rounding in mathematics has specific rules we follow, so everyone rounds the same. We round numbers to an identified place value. The digit in the place immediately to the right is used to round. If the digit is 5, 6, 7, 8, or 9, we round the number up. If the digit is a 1, 2, 3, or 4, then we round down. If the number is 0, it is already rounded, and we leave it the same.

For instance, let's look at the number 78. I want to round 78 to the 10s place. What digit is in the 10s place? (7). So, I want to look at the digit to the right of the 7. This digit is an 8. Do we round an 8 up or down? (Up). What is the next 10s place up from 70? (80).

Exploring

Mr. Young: Talk with your neighbor to explain why you think we use 5 as the rounding point. Why don't we use 4 or perhaps 6? (Wait time while pairs discuss)

Let's hear some thinking. (Mr. Young calls on various students.)

Student A: It's halfway.

Mr. Young: Halfway? You need to tell me more.

Student A's Partner: Well, if I'm adding to 10, then I have the facts: 0 plus 10, 1 plus 9, 2 plus 8, and so on. When one side goes up by 1, the other side goes down by 1. But, 5 plus 5 has the two sides equal.

Student B: If you think about it, you have 0, 1, 2, 3, and 4. Then, you have 5, 6, 7, 8, and 9.

(The mathematics coordinator enters the classroom and moves to stand beside some of the students. The class continues.)

Mr. Young: That is some very good thinking and just what mathematicians have discussed. Then, so everyone would use the same rule for rounding, the decision was made that 5 and higher round up and 4 and lower round down.

Work with your neighbor to round these numbers to the nearest 10s place: 12, 68, 54, 39, and 40.

(Students work the rounding problems as the teacher and coordinator move around the room.)

Mr. Young: Students, when we worked combinations to 100, you identified a way for you to know if the second addend was greater than 50, less than 50, or equal to 50. I want you to get more precise. At the moment, we are only using combinations to 100, but we are going to round and estimate answers to problems much greater than 100. So, listen carefully.

I want you to get out your individual slates and markers. I am going to call out a number. Write down the number, round the number to the nearest 10s place, then use the rounded number to get an estimate of the addend to 100. For example, I say the number 43. I know the digit 4 is in the 10s place. I look to the right one place, and I see the digit 3. I know to round 3 down, so 43 rounds to 40. Now, what would I add to 40 to reach 100? (60) I write down 60.

Students, what is the precise answer? (57) That's exactly right. Remember, there are times for precise answers, and there are times for estimates. I used rounding to get 43 to 40. I used my mathematics skills to recognize the addend 60 is needed to reach 100, and I used estimating to know that my answer to 43 plus what equals 100 is about 60. Is 57 about 60? (Yes)

OK, let's work together on your boards. Write down the number 74. Now, round 74 to the nearest 10s place. Show me what you wrote. Now, estimate the answer for the second addend to reach 100. Write it down, and show me. (30)

Now, we are ready. I'll call off the number, and you round and then estimate: 27, 85, 77, 12, 53, 60. (Students continue with slates.)

Summarizing

What is the rule we use to round?
When might we use rounding?
How does rounding help us with estimating?

Daily Analysis

Students demonstrated a clear understanding of how to round. A few students struggled with the place value names. Most students were weak in explaining how rounding was useful.

Daily Reflection

Mr. Young knew he needed to continue to focus on estimating as a mathematics skill. Too many of his students confused rounding as the same thing rather than one tool. He sent an e-mail to the coordinator requesting a visit.

Day 3 Lesson: Rounding Continued

Setting the Stage

Mr. Young: Yesterday, we learned about rounding. Wait until I ask you to show me, then I want you to use your thumbs-up to round up or thumbs-down to round down like this (Mr. Young demonstrates signal). Round 37 to the nearest 10s place. I think, 3 is in the 10s place. I look to the place to the right, and I see a 7. And, 7 is rounded up, so 37 is rounded to 40—I do a thumbs-up.

OK, let's try. Wait until I say, "Show me." First, 81. Show me (most thumbs are down). Next, 68. (Mr. Young waits slightly longer.) Show me. (Thumbs are up.)

Rounding works for any size number, and we can round to any place we choose. The same rules apply, so let's look at three-digit numbers. Look at the number 483. What places are in 483? (1s, 10s, and 100s) Very good. What if I wanted to round to the 10s place? Could you do this? Talk with your partner and see what you can do.

(Mr. Young calls on students to explain.)

What do you think the answer would be if I wanted to round to the 100s place? Work with your partner to get an answer.

(Mr. Young calls on several partner groups to explain.)

Would these same rules work if we had 1,000s? What about 10,000s?

Exploring

Mr. Young: Class, here are 10 numbers that range from 100s to 10,000s. I want you to read the directions, round to the correct place, and then write down your answer. Work two problems, and then share your answers with your partner. If you agree, move to the next two problems. If you disagree, raise your hand. (Mr. Young moves about the room checking students' work.)

(The principal again drops by with his walk-through visit.)

Summarizing

Mr. Young: Students, get out a clean sheet of paper. Write down what you know about rounding. Be sure to include what rules you know. Then, round the number on the whiteboard to the 1,000s place, and explain on your paper how you worked the problem.

Daily Analysis

Mr. Young grouped the students' papers into three stacks: high, middle, and low. He then assigned a number grade between 1 and 10 with 10 being high. Most of his students were either high or middle. He had five students score low, and two of these five rounded incorrectly. The remaining three students just did not have sufficient explanation.

Daily Reflection

Mr. Young knew he had to focus on the five students during the next lesson. He really was not sure if the students did not understand or just did not try.

Day 4 Lesson: Greater, Lesser, or Equal

Setting the Stage

Mr. Young: Class, we have been studying estimating, rounding, place value, and 100 as a benchmark. Today, we are going to put this knowledge together to do two things. First, we want to compare and order two numbers, and then we want to estimate an answer for an addition or subtraction problem.

Given two numbers of any size, they can be related in one of three ways. The first number can be greater than the second number, less than the second number, or equal to the second number. Do you think this is true? Think about this for a few minutes, and be ready to agree or disagree and explain your thinking.

OK, class, who wants to support agree? Raise your hand. Linda, what do you think?

Linda: I think "agree," because if I have two numbers like 4 and 5, then 4 is less than 5. If I have 7 and 3, then 7 is bigger than 3. Then, I could have 4 and 4 or 6 and 6, and they are the same.

Mr. Young: Good example, Linda. Who wants to explain their thinking for disagree? Tommy?

Tommy: Well, I think it works with the numbers we are using, but I don't think it will always work. What about fractions or really small numbers? My father told me that he had negative numbers in school.

Mr. Young: Tommy, that is very reasonable thinking. We haven't studied all the different numbers, especially negative ones yet. I want you to look at the number line that is above the whiteboard. Our number line starts at zero, and then goes to the right. Tommy, how far does it go to the right?

Tommy: 1,000.

Mr. Young: That's right, but do our numbers stop at 1,000?

Tommy: No, they keep on going.

Mr. Young: That's right. So, Tommy, pick a number from the number line.

Tommy: I chose 656.

Teacher: Good, now Tommy, can you pick a number that isn't less (to the left), greater (to the right), or equal to 656?

Tommy: No.

Mr. Young: Tommy, when you work on fractions and even negative numbers, you are going to find the same thing because they fit on a number line too.

(The coordinator drops by again. The class continues.)

Exploring

Mr. Young: Class, after looking at the number line, we know that the relation between two numbers is greater than, less than, or equal. How can we use what knowledge we have to determine their relationship?

I'm giving you two numbers: 4,537 and 7,362. Work with your partner to decide which number is greater and why.

(Mr. Young asks the coordinator to help him monitor students and watch for misconceptions.)

Mr. Young: Who would like to answer the question? OK, Tommy.

Tommy: 7,362 is bigger because it has 7 thousands compared to 4 thousands.

Mr. Young: That is exactly right. So, what place did you look at to get an answer?

Tommy: The 1,000s.

Mr. Young: Good thinking. Class, what if I had two numbers that had the same number of 1000s, such as 3,544 and 3,278?

Talk with your partner to make a decision.

(Class decides you would look at the 100s place.)

Mr. Young: OK, class, work with your neighbor to answer the following:

489 and 501

1,873 and 2,045

4,456 and 4,711

7,730 and 7,743

Mr. Young: In the problems we just worked, we used the phrases *is greater than, is equal to,* or *is less than.* You know mathematicians use symbols to represent mathematical ideas. We have been using the equal sign for some time. Can anyone tell me the phrase we can substitute for *is equal to?* Yes, Bobby.

Bobby: We can say, "Is the same as."

Mr. Young: Very good, Bobby. We use that phrase because some people confuse *equal* to mean *identical.* We can say 4 equals 2 plus 2, and see that 4 is the same as 2 plus 2, but the sides are not identical. Mathematicians also have symbols for *is greater than,* and *is less than.*

Now, I want you to use your knowledge in estimating an answer by rounding. Look at the four sets of numbers we just compared. What if they were addition problems? How could you use your knowledge to estimate an answer? Think on your own about the first one, and then we will discuss it.

If I wanted to round 489 to the 100s place, what would I get, class? (In unison, 500) What about 501 rounded to the 100s place? (In unison, 500)

Who can help me understand how this information can help me estimate an answer to this addition problem?

Billy:	After I rounded, I could add the two rounded numbers and get 1,000. My answer ought to be about 1,000.
Mr. Young:	Is 1,000 an exact answer or an estimated answer?
Billy:	Estimated.
Mr. Young:	Thanks for explaining, Billy. Good thinking. I want everyone to work the second and third problems on your own.

Summarizing

How does knowledge about place value help you compare two numbers?
How can rounding help you solve problems?
Where might you use rounding other than in the classroom?
How can rounding help you estimate?
For homework, I want you to think about this question and answer it the best you can. You can ask your parents for their ideas.
Is rounding always the best way to estimate an answer?

Daily Analysis

Mr. Young, based on the lesson, knew the students could round. He needed to help improve the students' writing abilities.

Daily Reflection

Mr. Young knew he wanted his students to see the value of rounding as well as increase their ability to make reasonable estimates using various strategies. He needed to provide the students with real-world examples of rounding from newspapers.

Day 5 Lesson: Game and Assessment

Setting the Stage

Mr. Young:	Students, we have been working with rounding as one tool to help you become better mathematics estimators. In life, it is important to have a sense about whether an answer is reasonable. You don't want to go shopping and buy a $20 item that is on sale for 25% off and then end up paying more than $20 because the sales clerk made a mistake. We have also been working with place value and using place value to round as well as compare the size of two numbers.
	As a way to help you improve your understanding, you have two tasks today. First, you are going to play a game. Second, you are going to answer several questions for me

independently, so I can understand what you know. The game is "I Have—Who Has?" and you have played it before. I am going to form you into groups of six. Each group will have a deck of cards that they shuffle and deal out facedown. The group leader will start by asking the "Who Has?" statement on the card.

(Turning on the overhead) Here are the groups with the first person being the group leader. Go ahead, and arrange your desks.

Exploring

Students play "I Have—Who Has?" by dealing out the cards (see examples provided and explanation). After 20 minutes, the game is stopped, and students return to their original organization. The game is explained in Figure 6.1.

Summarizing

Mr. Young: OK, class, settle down. Now, I am going to hand out a sheet of paper to each of you to work on independently. I want you to watch your time, but answer the questions the best you can. The more you write, the better I can understand what you mean. I'll let you know about the time remaining.

Figure 6.1   I Have—Who Has?

Game Directions: Each question pair is placed on a card. Students are formed into groups of four to six. Each group receives one set of cards. The cards are turned facedown and shuffled. All cards are dealt to the students, so each student will have more than one card. One student begins with the "Who Has?" statement, and then the student who is holding the card with the correct answer responds with the answer and then reads his or her question. The game continues until the group leader answers the last question.

I have 4,100.
Who has 3,075 rounded to the nearest 100?

I have 3,100.
Who has the symbol for *greater than*?

I have >.
Who has the missing addend of 100 for 43?

I have 57.
Who has the missing addend of 100 for 72?

I have 28.
Who has the symbol for *less than?*

I have <.
Who has 632 rounded to the 10s place?

I have 630.
Who has 5,199 rounded to the 1000s place?

I have 5,000.
Who has 85,492 rounded to the 10,000s place?

I have 90,000.
Who has a 7 in the 100s place?

I have 4,766.
Who has a 9 in the 1,000s place?

I have 89,021.
Who has 945 rounded to the 1,000s place?

I have 1,000.
Who has 4,149 rounded to the 100s place?

Mr. Young hands out the assessment (Figure 6.2).

Figure 6.2 Assessment

1. Round 5,712 to the nearest 1,000s place.

2. Round 12,469 to the nearest 100s place.

3. Round 56,123 to the nearest 10,000s place.

4. The number 1,450 was rounded to the nearest 10s place. What number could it have been before rounding?

   A. 1,455   B. 1,475
   C. 1,500   D. 1,454

(Continued)

(Continued)

5. Insert the correct mathematical symbol that makes the statement true:

6,127	5,998
14,562	15,001
7,254	7,554

6. If I go to the mall and buy two items that cost $27.99 each, what is a reasonable estimate of what I will spend? Explain your thinking.

7. If I am going to add 3,278 and 4,875, what is a reasonable estimate of the answer? Explain how you arrived at your estimate.

8. Why is being able to estimate important to mathematicians?

Weekly Lesson Analysis

Mr. Young graded his students' work. First, he graded problems 1 through 5. He checked the problems worked correctly and left problems worked incorrectly unmarked. With 25 students in his class, he then quickly scanned to see if there was any particular pattern. He noted that problem number 4, the one that provided the rounded number, was missed seven times.

As for the remaining problems 1 through 5, he could find no pattern. Although students missed some of the problems, the same student did not miss all of them.

Now, Mr. Young read through every paper for the problems 6 through 8. He wanted to get a general feel for what his class was thinking before grading the individual problems.

He decided that, for problem number 6, the estimation of the cost of two items, he would accept $50 or $60 as long as the students offered reasonable explanations. On problem 7, he expected the students to answer 8,000. Mr. Young knew he had to check for evidence that the student added and then rounded. If he found this, no credit would be given.

Problem 8 was really designed to see if the students could express themselves. He hoped to get an insight into their thinking. Furthermore, he recalled the classroom events of the last few days and the student responses. He attempted to determine if there were inconsistencies between his observations and the assessment performances.

As most students did well on the assessment, he decided he did not need to chart the problems or conduct an item analysis for incorrect answers except for problem 4. Problem 4 was the only item with multiple-choice answers. Of the seven students who missed problem 4, five of them selected answer C (1,500). The remaining two students selected answer A (1,455).

Weekly Lesson Reflection

Mr. Young was pleased with the assessment results. Although a few students appeared to be struggling, most students clearly passed the assessment. With the exception of problem 4, the first 5 problems were either right or wrong, and most students were right. He would need to check to be sure, but his guess was the students who missed number 4 probably did not read the question and just rounded 1,450. When he selected that answer, he really hadn't considered that possibility. He would check again to see which students missed problem 4 and if they were students with reading difficulties.

As for questions 6 and 7, he felt the students did get the idea of estimating. He needed to keep working with reasonableness of answers. The students who selected $50 as the answer did not round, and he was pleased to see that was the case. In the past, he had observed students round without thinking, and he did not want that happening.

Question 8 was interesting. He definitely needed to help students become better at writing, which in his mind meant they needed to be better at thinking. So, what did he know?

At this point, he reviewed the two forms he had concerning the mathematical practices. From the assessment, he felt that, as he started planning his next lesson series, he needed to do the following:

- Include more time for thinking and explaining
- Increase time for writing, and provide examples
- Review and use place value names
- Visit with the coordinator about the forms, CCSS, and planning

From the forms, he decided he needed to push his students toward better communication of their ideas and more discussion. He really needed to find some challenging problems the students could work on in groups of three or four. He believed his students were ready. He made a note to e-mail the mathematics coordinator and to search on the Internet.

(The principal and the coordinator later met to discuss the overall school progress on increasing levels of student engagement.)

QUESTIONS FOR DISCUSSION

On the Sequence Chart, what strategies has Mr. Young mastered?

On the Sequence Chart, what strategies do you think Mr. Young should work on next?

On the Proficiency Matrix, where do you think Mr. Young's students are performing?

On the Proficiency Matrix, what proficiencies should Mr. Young work on with his students?

What parts of the various lessons are routinely used in your school?

What parts of the various lessons are not frequently used at your school?

Are there parts of the different lesson components that should be incorporated into your school?

7 Building Support for Collegial Relationships

Leaders must lead by example. Shared leadership provides clear evidence of trust and respect. A positive relationship between teachers and their leaders, as well as among teachers, is critical to successful implementation of the CCSS. Trust, collegiality, involvement, and support all influence the motivation of teachers to the extent to which they are willing to try new ideas and make changes in classroom practices. With collegiality, teachers can engage in ongoing professional dialogues, share instructional strategies that work, and become collaborative partners with each other and their leaders to put the CCSS into practice. Teachers working together with their leader not only have support to change but also gain a high level of commitment to execute change. With trust and assistance, teachers are more willing to take risks and experiment with new ideas as their colleagues encourage, provide crucial feedback, and network with them. To forge relationships and build rapport, leaders and teachers should consider collegiality as a key feature of successful change.

Collegiality is a professional interaction among teachers and leaders with the purpose of learning from each other to develop expertise together. Collegiality is a break from the isolation of teachers working and learning on their own. To promote collegial relationships, leaders and their leadership teams can plan opportunities for teachers to work together by structuring face-to-face meeting times, thus allowing teachers to exchange ideas. Having time to get together and talk will help a majority of teachers not feel alone or isolated with needed instructional changes required by the CCSS. Because teachers and leaders can learn so much from each other, collegiality can be thought of as a move toward "we together can figure this out" versus " you have to learn about and implement the standards on your own." Collegiality can also mean, but is not limited to, collaborative planning, collaborative teaching, peer coaching, and collaborative research. Collegial teachers and leaders cooperate and communicate well with each other. With collegial relationships, successful change in classrooms can be achieved.

Although there are no magical recipes for forging collegial relationships and support, there are key principles leaders and leadership teams should consider. These key principles include the following:

- Building trust and self-confidence in teachers
- Supporting teachers
- Providing ongoing professional learning opportunities to meet the needs of every teacher
- Keeping teachers focused on maintaining the change and managing the journey
- Keeping confidences
- Providing respect
- Promoting professional learning communities
- Inspiring teachers

These key principles provide guidance to leaders and leadership teams as they work through the recommended activities contained within this book. Each of the key principles is explained in the following sections.

BUILDING TRUST AND SELF-CONFIDENCE IN TEACHERS

In order to build trust and self-confidence in all teachers, leaders and leadership teams must have an appreciation and respect for each staff member. Trust is the foundation of all positive collegial relationships and is one of the strongest bonds that can exist between teachers and leaders. With trust, teachers feel that they are able to rely on the leader and feel confident in the direction in which they are headed. With trust, teachers can cooperatively work with colleagues and take risks.

In a collegial setting, leaders value, validate, and inspire all teachers, thus building trust. With collegiality, teachers value and inspire each other. With trust and collegiality, change is easier and more comfortable to achieve. By having an initial trust, leaders and leadership teams can explain the rationale for how and why the standards will help students in mathematics as well as what teachers are expected to do as they prepare for the change process. With trust, teachers are allowed to contribute ideas to begin shifting toward the CCSS. Effective leaders express confidence in teachers as they begin a change process, thus instilling even more trust. Along the way, teachers should be given credit for the plans they create and the steps they take to incorporate the standards philosophy into daily lessons and instruction. Leaders share credit for all accomplishments, ideas, and contributions made by staff members. Building trust and confidence in teachers supports the interaction of colleagues and staff as they engage in a course of action to implement the CCSS.

SUPPORTING TEACHERS

Supportive leadership is the opposite of autocratic leadership. Supportive leaders are visible, accessible, and always there for teachers. Supportive leaders share leadership responsibilities. Considering the needs of all teachers with concern for their welfare is a key strategy for a supportive leader. Supportive leadership works well when the work of teachers becomes stressful or immediate changes in curriculum, instruction, or assessments are required. By providing empathy and support when teachers are anxious about a change initiative, a leader can win trust. To win this trust, leaders must be good listeners. To be supportive, leaders need to know when teachers need support and when they do not. When teachers actually need support, leaders and leadership team members must be visible, accessible, and able to provide assistance as they request help. Supportive leaders help teachers find their greatness. Every school, division, district or campus has teachers with talents, skills, experience, and expertise. Supportive leaders can help teachers channel the best ideas that will benefit students in mathematics.

PROVIDING ONGOING PROFESSIONAL LEARNING OPPORTUNITIES

All teachers need professional learning to acquire a rich mathematical background of content knowledge including number theory and algebra, geometry and measurement, probability and data analysis, as well as state-of-the-art instructional strategies required by CCSS. Leaders and leadership teams must provide ongoing professional learning opportunities to meet the needs of every teacher, keeping in mind that one-size professional learning does not fit all teachers. Professional development best occurs when staff learning is differentiated for varied purposes, interests, and career stages. The professional development needed for every teacher must be relevant to the standards and school goals and must focus on content knowledge, instructional delivery, and assessment of and for student learning. Leaders must remember that professional learning for teachers should always reflect back to the students and their achievements.

KEEPING TEACHERS FOCUSED ON MAINTAINING THE CHANGE

With the intention of maintaining a spotlight on the CCSS, leadership teams must keep the goal in the forefront for all teachers. Communicating regularly helps reinforce the target. Leaders must be able to effectively communicate the purpose of the standards and what it means for students. Teachers need to be reminded what the goal is, what is expected of them, and what they must do to make changes. When asked, each and every teacher in the school should be able to explain the CCSS and what he or she will personally be doing to bring about the change in mathematical content and instruction. Communications with and among teachers can maintain the vision for the CCSS via bulletin boards, electronic newsletters, and e-mail message reminders. Leaders and leadership teams should communicate often and review accomplishments on an ongoing basis, recalling that both verbal and nonverbal communication matters. Successful leaders are honest about the overall direction and any information teachers need to successfully and skillfully carry out their responsibilities. In managing the journey, time is required for the majority of staff members to deal effectively with change. Wise leaders remember to be patient, as change is a process and not an event. Forging collegial relationships with teachers is not a single event but is accomplished through the school year over time.

KEEPING CONFIDENCES

Teachers may have fears and concerns about their lack of problem-solving skills, mathematics content knowledge, or instructional strategies. As teachers try new approaches and unfamiliar instructional strategies described in the CCSS, they may need to confide in leaders or leadership team members who can be trusted to maintain confidentiality. Teachers need to have opportunities to share what is working and what is not. Leaders do not embarrass teachers or talk about them to other teachers, parents, or students. Leaders keep confidences that promote the value of trust and respect throughout the school.

PROVIDING RESPECT

Teachers who are treated with respect usually respond with high regard for others as well as take action for necessary changes for the CCSS. Providing respect means treating all teachers the same, so they feel that they are regarded fairly and equally. Leaders who provide respect for teachers include all teachers in meetings, discussions, and professional learning about the CCSS. While not every teacher will participate in every activity, effective leaders invite and include anyone willing to participate. For real inclusion, teachers need to feel a connection to the plan and action steps that are leading to the accomplishment of the CCSS by having access to input through leadership team representation. Part of providing respect includes praise and feedback for teachers. Teachers need to understand the process and know how they are doing in order to successfully achieve required changes for the CCSS.

PROMOTING PROFESSIONAL LEARNING COMMUNITIES

A professional learning community (PLC, different from leadership teams) is a team of teachers working together with a common vision to accomplish a goal. In a collegial school, shared leadership among teachers and their leader is widely found in the building. Teachers tend to motivate each other and seem to spread the leadership throughout the school. In a PLC, the majority of teachers want to learn best practices and grow their professional knowledge. The teachers want to create specific plans to ensure the changes for CCSS become a reality and want a sense of being on the right track in meeting the learning needs of every student. The PLC is an opportunity for teachers to collaboratively share skills and experiences that promote student achievement as well as involve teachers in decision making for the school.

INSPIRING TEACHERS

Effective leaders not only help teachers feel important but also help teachers believe and know they can accomplish and achieve more than they may have ever dreamed possible. To do this, leaders can pay attention to how teachers are managing change and let them know they are doing a good job. Leaders can also provide positive recognition that helps teachers feel important and spur them to continue the progress. Recognition and praise can be written or can be made publicly. To praise via writing, teachers can be thanked for the steps taken that are making a difference for students. For public praise, teachers can verbally be acknowledged for their efforts. Teachers should be given credit for their dedicated work in improving student achievement in mathematics. Effective working relationships inspired by their leader will form the cornerstone for success.

Following are two scenarios that may be helpful in furthering an understanding of how leaders can establish collegial relationships and support teachers.

SCENARIO 1: BASIC SKILLS

Carol, a seventh grade teacher, believes basic arithmetic skills are needed before students take any higher-level mathematics classes. Carol had always wanted to be a teacher and had entered the teaching profession after serving in the military. She decided her students should master multi-digit addition, subtraction, multiplication, and division problems along with basic fraction skills before she would open and teach using the district-adopted textbook. About a month after the school year began, Mr. Hyatt, the middle school assistant principal, decided to visit the classrooms of all six of the seventh grade mathematics teachers in his school. Using a five-minute walk-through form, he began noting the majority of teachers were focusing on the teaching of problem solving. Most of the teachers were using cooperative learning strategies and allowing students to talk to one another about the problems they were solving. Upon entering Carol's classroom, Mr. Hyatt noticed students sitting in rows quietly working on long division worksheets. Approximately half of the class had mastered long division skills but were required to continue the drills until everyone in the class was able to move on.

First come the questions: What should the principal do? Which of the previously listed key principle steps should be taken in this situation?

Considerations

Some perceptions may be helpful to consider. For example, the teacher's actions were a direct correlation to her belief that students must master computational skills. The teacher really wanted the class to stay together to help one another. Carol was an extremely popular teacher with the parents. She communicated via e-mail about student progress and often told parents how they could help their children with homework. She believed she was doing the right thing for her students.

Principal Actions

The assistant principal was completely taken by surprise in Carol's lack of instructional change. After all, he had initiated a PLC for the seventh grade teachers to help support each other. Judging by their discussion at the last meeting, he thought all teachers were on their way to implementing changes for the CCSS.

After much thought, Mr. Hyatt responded to Carol by stating, "I can see that you want all of your students to master basic arithmetic skills, and your use of worksheets has provided multiple problems of practice. I do, however, need to remind you of our school goal. We have adopted the CCSS. I know you want your students to be prepared for their futures. I believe you can do that by starting with the CCSS and the eight Standards for Mathematical Practice. Carol responded that she was not sure what to do as she had always spent the first semester with worksheet drills she personally created. Mr. Hyatt further indicated that he knew Carol could accomplish anything she set out to do. Mr. Hyatt said he would help her.

In order to build trust and rapport, Mr. Hyatt decided he would respect Carol, not saying anything negative to the other teachers about her lack of progress in initiating the standards. He also decided to ask her to reread the eight mathematical practices and have a discussion with him the following week. After processing what had happened in Carol's room, Mr. Hyatt recognized that not all teachers make instructional changes at the same rate. He realized that providing feedback to his teachers would be necessary.

The next week, Carol met with Mr. Hyatt to discuss the standards. Carol admitted that changing instruction would not be easy for her, but she would do what she was asked to do. Although she had participated in a professional learning session on the eight mathematical practices, she had not implemented any of them. Mr. Hyatt asked Carol to begin allowing students to talk with each other as they attempted to solve a problem-solving situation.

Within two weeks, Carol found that students were enjoying talking to one another about how they began to solve a problem. She found they were on task. Carol indicated students were learning so much from each other.

Mr. Hyatt could not resist reminding Carol that she too could learn powerful strategies from her colleagues. He reminded her that the PLC meetings with her team would be an invaluable help to her as she continued to incorporate the eight CCSS student practices. Collaboration and support from and with her colleagues would make a difference.

Mr. Hyatt's high expectations for Carol seemed to spur her to be able to transform her classroom. He learned that Carol had not previously understood the goals for the CCSS and therefore could not implement the desired approaches. Mr. Hyatt learned that he would need to continue monitoring all teachers, providing ongoing reminders of why these standards were critical to student success. He discovered that he must ensure that teacher collaboration was truly occurring.

SCENARIO 2: WORKING ALONE

Ryan, a third grade teacher, did not want to work with other teachers. He told the mathematics coach, Ms. Lewis, that the building principal should be the leader and that shared leadership was "not his thing." He stated, "The principal should tell us what she wants us to do, and then I'll do it. I don't have time for meetings as I need to use my time wisely to grade papers and make copies for student practice."

First, here are the questions: What should the leadership team (or mathematics coach or specialist) do? Which of the previously listed key principle steps should be taken in this situation?

Considerations

The leadership team's reaction was to first seek understanding of why Ryan did not want to work with others. They decided to ask him up front, and he replied, "The other two third grade teachers are women. They stick together and really don't listen to what I say when we have planned together in the past. They are just not interested in what I could contribute. Besides that, the principal's job is to lead, not mine. I was hired to teach."

Leadership Team Actions

The leadership team decided to select one member of the team, Ms. Lewis, to work with Ryan. Ms. Lewis decided to schedule a consultation with him. She told him that she understood what had previously occurred with his grade-level team. Ms. Lewis informed Ryan she would be participating in the next PLC meeting.

At the next PLC meeting, Ms. Lewis suggested that collegiality is a key feature of successful change at their school. She told the team they would be surprised how much they could learn together and support each other's efforts for the eight CCSS student practices. She stated, "Each member of the team has good ideas. Each member of the team must be professional, listening carefully to potential new approaches. You were each hired to make a difference for our students, and each of you matters."

With Ms. Lewis present, the third grade PLC meeting went well. She decided to be visible and accessible at other team meetings in the future. She assured the teachers that their time spent in collaboration was worth it and was greatly appreciated. Apparently, the other two women teachers previously believed Ryan was not interested in the goal of incorporating the CCSS student practices and had ignored him. With lengthy conversations and much studying, Ms. Lewis was able to help the team focus on a sense of urgency about the new student practices. Soon, all three third grade team members were able to articulate the vision and were able to identify things they could do to improve student achievement. It all started with sitting around the table face-to-face, listening respectfully, and staying on task. The team began communicating daily, trying new strategies. They found they could rely on the mathematics coach for support and inspiration.

Finally, concerning the principal, Ryan learned that shared leadership is how schools can transform. He learned to look forward to collaborative planning and was glad he was able to impact the decisions the team made to improve student achievement. For the first time, he believed he was an important member of the school team.

SUMMARY: BUILDING SUPPORT FOR COLLEGIAL RELATIONSHIPS

Trust is a significant factor in change. Trust is built over time through working collegially. Teachers must feel appreciated, respected, involved, and supported in order to voluntarily undertake significant change, especially change involving classroom instructional strategies. Trust is built when leaders maintain confidences. Trust is built when leaders and leadership representatives know enough information about teachers to provide the correct professional development at the necessary time. Trust is built when all staff speak with confidence about goals and desired outcomes, carefully listen to teachers, and still maintain high ideals and expectations that focus on student success.

QUESTIONS FOR DISCUSSION

When considering the principles of building support, what are the most important in your opinion and why?

Of the principles, which one (or ones) should be a major focus at your school?

What actions are necessary for you to take to support the identified principle?

In Scenario 1: Basic Skills, what do you think was done correctly?

In Scenario 1: Basic Skills, what would you recommend be done?

In Scenario 2: Working Alone, what do you think was done correctly?

In Scenario 2: Working Alone, what would you recommend be done?

8 Maintaining Support to Increase Implementation

Introducing, maintaining, and achieving instructional change is a long-term investment for leaders and teachers. As presented in previous chapters, adults adopt change at different rates and for different reasons. One vitally important job for mathematics leaders and leadership teams is to provide the needed support to the correct teachers at the appropriate times. If this is to happen, teacher monitoring must occur.

Readers can readily recognize that Mr. Young in Chapter 6 will need different support than some of the other teachers. Leaders and leadership teams need to know how many "Mr. Young" types are at the campus. Leaders waste valuable time, energy, and talent when they insist that Mr. Young sit through introductory sessions concerning the CCSS practices. Leaders and leadership teams need to purposefully utilize Mr. Young.

SUPPORT VERSUS EVALUATION

Leaders, especially those responsible for evaluation, must clearly understand the distinction between support and evaluation. Formal school leaders need to be highly involved in supportive measures to adopt and implement the CCSS and the mathematical practices. While leaders need to coordinate and collaborate with other staff to provide support, they are the ones ultimately responsible for results and progress.

When implementing or learning something new, teachers need support. Whether it is new content or new instructional strategies, each teacher has a learning curve (as outlined by Figure 3.1) that progresses from novice to master to expert. *Innovations, Initiatives, Strategies, or Programs Adoption Process* (Figure 8.1) clearly indicates the natural formation of leadership teams

Figure 8.1 Innovations, Initiatives, Strategies, or Programs Adoption Process

Event	Usage	Level of Use
Research, review, selection	• Nonuse	• 0
Introduction	• Nonuse	• 0 to I
Initial training	• use – initiators • nonuse – all others (nonadopters/rejecters)	• II to III • 0, I, II
Monitor with feedback, support (multiple episodes)	• use – initiators • use – earlier adopters • nonuse – later adopters rejecters, resisters	• III to IVA • II to III • 0, I, II • 0, I
Continued training, monitoring with feedback, support (multiple episodes, differentiated)	• use – initiators • use – early adopters • use – later adopters • nonuse – rejecters/ resisters	• IVB to V • IVA to IVB • III to IVA • 0, I, II
Continued training, monitoring with feedback, support (multiple episodes differentiated by need)	• use – initiators • use – early adopters • use – later adopters • nonuse – resisters	• V to VI • V to VI • IVB to V • 0, I, II
Continued training, monitoring with feedback, support (multiple episodes differentiated by need)	• use – initiators • use – early adopters • use – later adopters • nonuse – resisters	• VI • VI • V to VI • 0, I, II

Decision Point With Resisters

Event	Usage	Level of Use
Direct intervention strategies for resisters	• use – no longer resisting • nonuse	• III • 0, I. II

(Resisters electing to adopt after direct intervention will need continued support through levels of use III, IVA, IVB, V, and VI. If resisters remain—highly unlikely—they need to be transferred or terminated.)

0 = nonuse; I = orientation; II = preparation; III = mechanical use; IVA = routine; IVB = refinement; V = integration; and VI = renewal (Hall & Hord, 2001, p. 82)

and, perhaps, study groups as use of the innovation builds across the campus. If there is no support for learning and practicing, there is no progress. This failure in understanding is why many of the current approaches to professional development do not transfer into classrooms. There is a significant gap between knowledge and application.

After carefully reviewing and discussing Figure 8.1, leaders and leadership teams can better understand the dynamics of change. Moving down the Event column indicates actions for training and implementation of a strategy or innovation. The Usage column indicates the degree of implementation by the adopting groups of initiators, earlier adopters, and later adopters. The third column provides the Level of Use from research by Hall and Hord (2001). The levels 0 to VI are labeled at the end of the table.

Leaders and leadership teams can observe the degree of implementation through the levels of use as each adopting group moves through proficiency with the strategy or innovation. Further, leaders and leadership teams are aware of the interests and training needs as the groups make progress. Other than initial training for base-level knowledge, the professional development opportunities are not one size fits all.

Evaluation is the process of rating someone against a set of norms or standards. It is used as a method of quality control. In order to remain as a teacher, coordinator, principal, or in another job responsibility, one must surpass or at least equal the minimum requirements. While perhaps not impossible, it is certainly extremely difficult to develop positive change through evaluation. As a general rule, unless an individual is operating below standard, evaluation is not geared toward improvement or change. Our message on this has been consistent. Teachers have received formal evaluations for decades. If evaluations were going to change instructional practices, they would have done so by now.

When adopting change, teachers and leaders have two significant stages they must complete. First, they must engage in the appropriate practices described in the change. This stage is the early learning curve when the change (new strategy) is uncomfortable and awkward. As teachers and leaders engage in the required behaviors, they reach a comfort zone with the change. If the change is effective, then when teachers reach this comfort zone, student learning actually increases. With this increase in student learning, teachers move into the second stage, or empowerment. In empowerment, teachers can use the strategy with ease and actually begin making adaptations of the strategy that further increase student learning.

Many times within schools, teachers and leaders never even reach engagement with a strategy or change, much less empowerment. While intentional evaluation may achieve some degree of compliance, the strategy will not move beyond mere surface-level application. Support, not evaluation, addresses the learning curve and empowerment issue.

For example, perhaps teachers, with the approval of leaders, have received training on higher-order questioning. An evaluator enters the classroom, observes an appropriate amount of time, and then leaves. Several days later, the teacher receives a form in his or her box with a 2 circled on a 1 to 5 scale for asking higher-order questions. What exactly is the teacher to do with this information? How is he or she to improve? If just beginning this strategy, a 2 may actually be a good score, although the teacher will clearly not see it that way.

In support, the same lesson occurs. The visitor is moving about the room working with students and generally helping in the classroom. The teacher asks a couple of higher-order questions, but students do not respond very well. In this case, the visitor can discuss with the teacher the positive aspects of asking higher-order questions and focus on the student responses. "You asked a good question; how did the students respond? Students are adjusting to answering higher-order questions too. Do you recall anything from the training that may help them better formulate an answer?" The teacher may respond that he or she should have waited longer or allowed students to talk with partners.

DATA AND ASSESSMENTS

Leaders, to appropriately provide leadership, must be in classrooms collecting data. Other data, besides leader-collected data, are also needed. Periodic, common assessments can provide meaningful data for students, teachers, and leaders. Assessments need to focus on the content taught during the set time period. If at all possible, assessments should also focus on mathematical practices or NCTM process standards. For convenience, if the periodic assessments need to be multiple choice, then at intervals between the multiple-choice assessments, teachers need to provide open-ended, common assessments that are rubric scored.

Data are important when viewed as progress over time. Data are also important for alerting teachers and leaders of content and concepts in which students are underperforming. Chapter 4's Tier 1 RTI offered numerous suggestions for teachers to use in their classrooms. Leaders also need to know of these strategies. By having feedback that informs instruction in various forms, students have a much greater chance of receiving the help they need at the time they most need it.

CLASSROOM VISITS

The content and practices contained in the CCSS are not going to self-initiate with mathematics teachers. Leaders need to carefully and consistently monitor implementation. Monitoring will not be successful if classroom visits are not included in the overall strategic implementation plan. The positive news is that monitoring is not done, nor should be done, solely by leaders.

Teachers, central office staff, specialists, coaches, and leaders can conduct classroom visits for support. By sharing this responsibility, leaders are reinforcing the idea that the requested changes are important, and that support, not evaluation, during the change process is the goal. Leaders, however, are responsible for assuring that all participants clearly know and understand the rules for supportive classroom visits.

Classroom visits may occur in several ways. Combining the various ways offers the best analysis of true classroom conditions. Leaders and individuals assisting the leaders may use classroom visit tallies, targeted classroom visits, or classroom walk-throughs. Each type of visit process provides important information that can be used to support teachers during implementation as well as to identify areas needed for professional development.

Classroom Visit Tallies

An example of a classroom visit tally for teacher actions and student actions is provided in Figure 8.2. Leaders should immediately notice that teacher names are not placed on the form. As a reminder, these classroom visit types are nonevaluative. Individuals collecting this information are in classrooms for brief periods of time, one to three minutes, with the express purpose of looking for specific strategies and actions for supporting change.

Individuals collecting the data want to quickly visit as many mathematics classrooms as possible within an identified period of time. Classrooms may be visited more than once. For instance, an individual may have an opportunity to enter mathematics classes from 10:00 a.m. to 10:45 a.m. During this 45-minute time slot, both third and fourth grade teachers are teaching mathematics. If there are four teachers per grade level (eight total teachers), then the individual may visit 18 to 20 classrooms at two minutes each with some travel and recording time. With eight teachers, every teacher is visited twice and some three times.

The purpose is to gather a quick snapshot in every classroom at various points in the lesson. Tallies should not be made inside classrooms but in the hall as the visitor is moving to the next classroom. Visitors record only what they observed. For instance, the classroom teacher announces to

Figure 8.2 Classroom Visit Tally Forms

Classroom Visit Tally—Student Actions

School:_____Grade or Course:_____

Date: _____

Students are:	Classroom				
	CR1	CR2	CR3	CR4	CR5
Discussing mathematics					
Answering questions that extend mathematics (What if . . . ? What would happen . . . ?)					
Demonstrating understanding (oral, written, hands-on)					
Using a variety of tools in a lesson					
Working collaboratively in pairs					
Working collaboratively in small groups					
Sharing/explaining their thinking					
Using technology (calculators, computers)					
Engaging in classroom activities					
Investigating/exploring mathematical concepts					

Comments:

Classroom 1: _____

_____

Classroom 2: _____

_____

Classroom 3: _____

_____

Classroom 4: _____

_____

Classroom 5: _____

_____

(Continued)

(Continued)

Classroom Visit Tally—Teacher Actions

School:_____Grade or Course:_____

Date: _____

Teachers are:	Classroom				
	CR1	CR2	CR3	CR4	CR5
Encouraging discussion about mathematics • Students to students					
Encouraging discussion about mathematics • Teacher to students					
Asking higher-order questions					
Asking probing and scaffolding questions					
Providing engaging activities					
Using a variety of tools in lessons					
Using technology (calculators, computers)					
Providing wait time					
Using grouping strategies: • Pairs (think-pair-share, reciprocal)					
• Small groups (round-robin, jigsaw, lineups)					
Teaching with multiple representations					
Providing problem solving/exploration experiences					
Monitoring interactions (moving around the room, etc.)					

Comments:

Classroom 1: _____

_____

Classroom 2: _____

_____

Classroom 3: _____

_____

Classroom 4: _____

_____

Classroom 5: _____

_____

Source: From *A Guide to Mathematics Leadership: Sequencing Instructional Change*, by D. S. Balka, T. H. Hull, and R. Harbin Miles, 2009, Thousand Oaks, CA: Corwin. Copyright by Corwin. Reprinted with permission.

his or her class that the students are about to form into groups. Yet groups are not formed while the visitor is inside the classroom. As a result, the strategy of grouping is not recorded as being observed.

Visitors to the classrooms may use the student actions tally, the teacher actions tally, or both. Once the visits are completed, the tally pages should be dated and filed in a secure location, preferably with the school principal. Leaders are seeking patterns over a period of time. After several different individuals conduct numerous snapshots, leaders have data regarding which strategies are being used and which strategies are not being used.

Targeted Classroom Visits

Targeted classroom visits are conducted much like classroom visit tallies, only there is no particular form, and there is only one strategy being counted. Targeted visits can be used after professional development or after teacher conversations have been conducted concerning classroom visit tallies. Targeted visits last an extremely short period of time, usually less than one minute. The strategy is being used inside the classroom, or the strategy is not being used. However, leaders can quickly see that, with less than one minute per room, mathematics classrooms can be quickly visited numerous times within a short time duration.

Leaders can add a variation to the targeted classroom visit that includes staying longer in any classroom observed using the strategy. If the strategy is observed, the leader or visitor remains long enough to ensure the strategy is being used effectively.

Even though these visits are nonevaluative, some teachers will still be highly concerned, at least when the visits start. By using targeted visits of less than one minute, the visitor prevents teachers from quickly adjusting what they are doing to include the strategy they think the visitor wants to see.

Classroom Visit Walk-Throughs

Classroom visit walk-throughs focus longer periods of time within individual classrooms. Nonetheless, if at all possible, the period of time is shorter than anything required for evaluation. A list of questions visitors may consider for walk-throughs is provided below. Classroom visitors can learn a great deal about instruction and instructional strategies in a relatively brief period of time. These longer visits should probably not be used by leaders when they are first working with teachers to support change because they are so similar to evaluations. Also, leaders need to check to ensure that this process can be used without crossing over into evaluation. For visits of approximately seven minutes, teachers' names may be included on the form unless policies exist against such moves. Following is a list of what leaders can learn in seven minutes or less from a classroom visit:

- Is the lesson content appropriate or misaligned?
- Is the discussion teacher led or student oriented?
- Is the teacher located at the front or mobile?
- Are questions directed or open-ended?
- Are questions procedural or thinking?
- Are materials inflexible or adaptable?
- Is classroom management or student learning the focus?
- Are students providing short answers or thoughtful responses?
- Are students using textbooks and workbooks or a variety of materials?
- Are students subdued or animated?
- Is student involvement stratified or inclusive?
- Are students working independently or in groups?
- Are desks in stationary rows or flexible arrangements?

Readers need to consider these questions in light of visiting Mr. Young's classroom in Chapter 6. While a shorter visit time may not provide answers to each question, most of the questions can be covered. In the seven-minute time frame, these questions can be answered. Readers need to recall attention span and short-term memory research for children and young adults. Finally, readers must remember that these are trends, not mandates. Effective leaders are using multiple sources to gather data to support instructional shifts. The questions leaders are asking are not *always* or *never* but rather *adequate* and *appropriate*.

Leaders and leadership teams have been provided several ways to purposefully enter classrooms to monitor implementation and change. These methods are separate and apart from a leader's role of providing teacher evaluation. Individuals other than leaders are encouraged to use these forms and ideas as part of the monitoring process. Leaders will find it difficult to do these monitoring processes without leadership team assistance.

LEADERSHIP AND MANAGEMENT REQUIRED

Change can appear overwhelming and highly complex. Leaders and teachers, who perhaps are already struggling to keep what they have going, obviously are not overly excited with the prospect of doing things differently. Everyone needs to remember that, while change does take initial energy, after complete adoption, it takes no more energy than what is currently being used once the change has become routine and integrated. When the change initiative is directly related to student achievement, energy is actually saved in the future. When an effective instructional strategy (such as think-pair-share) is adopted, then more students successfully learn the mathematics content with better retention rates. This translates into fewer students needing reteaching, remediation, and constant review of past content.

For leaders, change requires both leadership and management skills. Leadership is needed to establish the need for change, set the vision, maintain the focus, build collaboration, provide support, and demonstrate progress. Management skills are needed to monitor implementation, collect and analyze data, and interpret the data.

Without management skills, adoption does not occur because there is no pressure. Without leadership skills, compliance may be achieved, but successful integration of the innovation into classroom routines that make a difference in student achievement will not.

For instance, management skills are required in visiting classrooms and collecting data concerning the degree of implementation being reached. Leadership skills are required when sharing the data with teachers to ensure positive, continued mastery of the strategy or innovation rather than a perceived punishment or threat.

SEPARATED ROLES

As discussed, entering classrooms for the purpose of supporting change is often an unclear task for leaders responsible for evaluation, coaches and supervisors not responsible for evaluation, and most important, the teachers receiving the visit. Distinguishing the difference is not nearly as difficult as it may first appear, but leaders must never blur the lines once they are established. The exception is with specific permission from the teacher involved.

If leaders pause to reflect, they realize that formal evaluations traditionally consist of a preconference, an observation, a postconference, and written documentation. During an evaluation, the leader sits in the back of the room and takes notes. For this reason, sitting in the back of the room taking notes is almost always associated with evaluation.

Classroom visits that are nonevaluative and for support require that the visitor never sit down, never take notes inside the classroom, and when possible, interact with students. Then, teachers clearly know when they are being evaluated and when they are being monitored for support. Leaders should also never use the same form for dual purposes of support and evaluation. The exception to this rule is when teachers request specific feedback from an observer whom they trust. The teachers, in this case, are seeking support for growth and improvement.

SHARING LEADERSHIP

Rarely are formal leaders able to launch and sustain significant, meaningful change initiatives by themselves. While formal leaders may decide it is just easier to go it alone, they will soon discover that success remains elusive. Change intended to directly improve student learning and achievement in mathematics is too complex for a single individual. The only logical option is for formal leaders to share responsibility and to empower teachers by forming some variation of collaborative leadership teams.

Forming a team, however, is not the ending action for leaders but the opening one. Leaders must provide leadership. Teachers willing to serve on leadership teams need guidance and clarity concerning their roles and responsibilities. Teachers, as members of a leadership team, build trust and communication and do not serve to evaluate colleagues. Leadership teams evaluate program implementation and student progress across schools, grade levels, or subject areas. Leadership teams must avoid focusing on individual teacher performance.

Providing Feedback on Visit Forms

Collecting data on classroom events has no positive benefits, only negative ones, if the data are not shared with teachers. While teachers do not need to see individual forms, they do need to see the totals from the forms as well as the forms being used. In fact, teachers should be involved in creating the forms and in establishing methods used to monitor progress on adoption and implementation. As recommended earlier, teachers should be trained to use the various forms and then allowed to collect data. Leaders are setting clear expectations when they articulate the program needs on a form. Teachers can assist leaders in being reasonable with their expectations.

Data are neutral. Data are not inherently good or bad. Adults interpret data and add positive or negative meaning. Leaders need to be aware of this. When providing feedback, leaders do not want to share their opinions about the data. If leaders state that they are "very disappointed" in the results, then teachers may feel compelled to respond accordingly. This is true regardless of how teachers may actually feel.

Leadership team members should present the data and allow teachers to respond. "I have totaled the visit forms from October 1 to October 23.

There were four individuals who collected this data during that period of time. What you see in the right-hand column is a ratio of the number of times the strategy was observed over the number of classroom visits. For instance, you notice that the strategy pair-share was observed four times out of 23 classes visited or 4/23. Read over the form results, and then share with me your thoughts."

At first, teachers may not feel free to discuss or may believe that "I used the strategy more; you just weren't there. People didn't stay in the room because I used it later." Discussion leaders need to be cautious of nonpositive conversations. They may acknowledge the teachers' feelings by stating that they are sure that the strategy was not recorded every time it was used. Discussion leaders then want to return to the present with, "When we met to discuss implementing the CCSS and the mathematical practices, we agreed that pair-share was an important strategy. Do you still feel it is important?" After a period of time for discussion, leaders want to ask teachers to state what should happen next.

Finally, to encourage teachers' conversations, discussion leaders may form the teachers into groups of two or three and let them discuss the forms and the results. Leaders should be open and honest about answering questions from teachers concerning the use of the data, even if leaders feel they have answered the same questions before.

SCENARIO 1: THE MIDDLE SCHOOL PRINCIPAL

A middle school principal, Mr. S, was concerned about the mathematics instruction occurring in his building. His state was increasing student expectations and altering the annual assessments to include open-ended questions. Early results indicated the students in his school were not going to perform well on the mathematics assessments. The instruction he observed was very traditional and teacher directed, with students listening.

Mr. S decided to seek help from the district curriculum director, who contacted a mathematics consultant. The curriculum director, mathematics consultant, and Mr. S met to outline their concerns. The curriculum director began the conversation by showing the consultant's state-developed documents concerning the changes coming to the mathematics year-end assessments. She stated that she held a meeting with all school principals to indicate the changes, and Mr. S soon called her asking about what changes to make.

The mathematics consultant asked the curriculum director and Mr. S what they thought classrooms needed to look like in order to meet these new state demands. Both individuals responded that students needed to be much more engaged and involved in lessons as well as having more opportunities to work together on more difficult mathematics problems. The mathematics consultant advised the curriculum director and Mr. S that the teachers needed to understand and accept that these changes in instruction were needed.

The mathematics consultant suggested that classroom visit tallies be used to help teachers move forward in changing instructional practices. A meeting was held with the mathematics teachers. The mathematics consultant, Mr. S, and the curriculum director led the session. The mathematics consultant encouraged the curriculum director to basically repeat her previous principal session with the teachers.

The teachers were receptive and studied the state documents. When asked what students needed to be able to do to perform well on the exam, teachers discussed several ideas, including working in groups. Mr. S asked if the teachers felt that they needed more training on collaborative grouping, and teachers assured him they did not.

Two weeks later, the mathematics consultant returned and trained the curriculum director and Mr. S on using the Classroom Visit Tally forms. He recommended that only the student actions form be used. He also asked Mr. S to discuss the process and form with his teachers. Teachers were provided an opportunity to ask questions and alter the form. No changes were suggested.

Soon after this meeting, Mr. S and the curriculum director began conducting classroom visits specifically looking for student engagement and collaborative grouping with student pairs or groups of three. After several weeks, the consultant returned and also conducted classroom visits. All data were compiled, and after 31 classroom visits, grouping was never observed. Furthermore, very few tallies were made indicating students were actually more engaged. Mr. S was very concerned about the scheduled teacher conversation over the form. The consultant agreed to attend, but he suggested to Mr. S that he remain as quiet as possible. He was to try to reflect the questions back to the teachers.

The teacher meeting started. Mr. S handed out the totals and asked teachers for their thoughts. Teachers immediately became animated. They said they were using the grouping strategy on a regular basis but that neither he nor the curriculum director was ever present. In their opinion, the form was just wrong. The consultant noticed that Mr. S was about to put an end to the conversation, so the consultant asked the teachers to recommend changes to the form. The consultant said, "When you first reviewed the form, you supported these strategies. Now, you have had a chance to work with them. Which strategies do you now think are not beneficial to students in mastering the upcoming state assessment?"

The teachers seemed hesitant to respond, so the consultant asked them to form into pairs and discuss the strategies. If the form was not accurate, it needed to be changed. The pair conversations became very lively and continued for eight to ten minutes before the consultant pulled the teachers back together. This time, teachers talked more about the form and the strategies. A few moderated word changes were offered by the teachers and readily accepted by Mr. S.

The consultant then asked the teachers to think about the following: "If 31 classes were visited at various times during the lesson and during various days of the week, do you think it is possible for a strategy being used by every teacher to never be observed?" The teachers began discussing the difficulties of grouping and why they were uncomfortable in using it. Now, the consultant and curriculum director were able to express empathy with starting a new strategy and offered to help make the transition. Teachers stated that they were willing to have the curriculum director and consultant help them with grouping strategies.

SUMMARY: MAINTAINING SUPPORT TO INCREASE IMPLEMENTATION

Teachers adapt to change at different rates. Leaders need to understand this human dynamic if they want to successfully move teachers forward in implementing the CCSS content and, more important, the Standards for Mathematical Practice in mathematics. To appropriately help teachers make the needed change, teachers need support during the learning process.

Appropriate support cannot be offered if leaders and those assisting leaders are not aware of the current level of adoption and usage for every teacher. While teachers can be grouped according to needs for professional development and additional training, the groupings are not successful without knowledge from the leaders and leadership teams about what teachers need to incorporate next.

QUESTIONS FOR DISCUSSION

Study Figure 8.1, *Innovations, Initiatives, Strategies, or Programs Adoption Process*. What does this mean for significant instructional change at your school?

How can Figure 8.2, *Classroom Visit Tally Forms*, be used effectively to promote change?

How can Figure 8.2, *Classroom Visit Tally Forms*, be misused and thwart change?

In Scenario 1: The Middle School Principal, what is the thought process from the principal's point of view?

In Scenario 1: The Middle School Principal, what is the result from the teachers' points of view?

In Scenario 1: The Middle School Principal, what could have been done differently to improve change?

9 Leading the Way for Change

I f the vision offered by the CCSS initiative is to become reality, it is leaders and leadership that will make it happen. Failure of previous initiatives has not been because of a lack of information or a scarcity of research; rather, failure is due to the inability to translate the intent of the research into purposeful classroom strategies and actions that support and encourage students' mathematical learning, along with the inability of leaders to build and sustain some functional form of leadership teams. The CCSS have clearly identified the content and the necessary mathematical practices. We have provided leaders with the translation of research into specific actions. Now, the future resides with the decisions leaders make and the actions leaders take.

A FORMULA FOR CHANGE

Generally, people resist change or at least try to avoid it when change is related to their careers. We usually find change to be uncomfortable when we are faced with having to do something outside of our daily work routines. Leaders who find themselves responsible for a major change initiative need to understand this dynamic of human nature regarding change. As pressure is exerted over time, change occurs. Pressure is the result of effort, and the formula can be written like this:

Time + Effort = Change

When considering change and trying to institute change, leaders may want to consider a slightly different version of this same formula—its negation:

No Time + No Effort = No Change

This format of the formula clearly helps leaders understand that, if they do not have the time or energy to devote to the change or have the time and energy to manage someone else in charge of the change, then the change is not important to teachers either. Why would teachers want to spend time and energy on a change when it is of no value to their leader? The fact is that they do not.

OVERCOMING RESISTANCE

In recalling earlier chapters, leaders know that, even when changes are considered important, requested changes tend to be routinely ignored or rejected. Resistance arises only when pressure is applied. If there is no pressure to adopt, there can be no resistance against the adoption. If change is adopted, effort over time must be provided. Many programs or initiatives have no serious effort or time attached and therefore never move beyond the ignored or rejected consideration. When change does not occur, if it is ever noticed, then the result is often translated as resistance.

WARNING OF *CAVEAT EMPTOR*

The first change formula stated above creates some tough decisions for leaders to face. There is a limit to resources, especially time. Leaders' time is limited, but so is the time for the teachers they are leading. Wasting time is a serious problem when we consider the heavy class loads of many teachers. When time is wasted in one area, it usually is taken from another area. Regardless of what leaders want to achieve, they must start with where they are and what they have. Shortcuts or miracle cures are not going to work.

As the pressure to implement the CCSS increases, leaders will confront an unbelievable number of program decisions. Many vendors will approach leaders with an offer of the "perfect" program. By purchasing the program, leaders will no longer need to be concerned about the CCSS because the publishers offer an "all-inclusive" deal. In addition, time is saved. This temptation to adopt the "perfect" program is difficult to resist.

However, leaders can decide to treat time as an investment. While it is true that good decisions may take some time originally, they are a wise investment and will grow with time being returned. Before jumping on any particular bandwagon, leaders need to consider three factors in screening programs.

SCREENING FACTORS

The screening factors are as follows:

1. Program selection

2. Program support

3. Program culture

Leaders have gained a great deal of knowledge if they have worked their way through our book. This knowledge can be used to guide their decisions. By not carefully considering these three factors, instructional leaders have practically guaranteed a lack of success and will undermine the strategies recommended throughout this book.

Program Selection

Selecting a program or initiative that is truly aligned to the identified need is quite obvious but also routinely overlooked. Assume leaders want to address the mathematics content from the CCSS and they want to encourage teachers to use strategies that promote the Standards for Mathematical Practice. When leaders are confronted with these decisions in the form of programs, they frequently focus on three factors: (1) On the surface, the program or initiative sounds reasonable; (2) it probably has had some level of reported success; and (3) the program is assumed to work. Meeting one or even all three of these factors does not provide adequate screening. A program or initiative that does not directly impact student achievement can be passed over before any other factor is considered.

Inherent Problems

Three rules of thumb arise when it comes to unsuccessful programs or initiatives. Leaders need to check to see if any of these rules are present. One rule is that the program or initiative is actually ineffective—it does not work. Ineffective programs may not work because they are not directly tied to the mathematics content students need to learn from the CCSS. They may also be ineffective due to certain requirements, such as that the program or initiative requires more time than is available, the program or initiative requires supporting strategies that are not intended to be used, or resource materials are not accessible. With these omissions, the program cannot be effective.

The second rule of thumb is that the program or initiative is effective but it does not address the identified CCSS content. In other words, it does assist students in learning mathematics, just not the mathematics contained in the CCSS. This situation is often difficult to determine from a surface-level review.

Finally, the third rule of thumb is the program or initiative does not work because it cannot be implemented under the current conditions. Implementation is a serious issue. During program or initiative screening, instructional leaders need to be able to clearly articulate the actions needed to ensure adequate implementation. If these actions cannot, or will not, be accomplished, the program or initiative, regardless of how effective it may be, should not be adopted.

What Should Leaders Do?

- Have all relevant parties study the research and the program or initiative.
- Ensure that there is an alignment between data specific to the identified need and division program goals.
- Ensure the data generated by the program or initiative are compatible to division- and school-level data.
- Pilot the program or initiative with reluctant volunteers. Willing volunteers tend to make the program or initiative successful in spite of its failings, while resistant participants will undermine the program in spite of its benefits. Leaders need accurate, honest, and unbiased results. (Hull, Harbin Miles, & Balka, 2011, p. 37)

Program Support

The difference between support for program implementation and teacher evaluation creates tremendous confusion. During the early stages of implementation of a program or initiative, teachers need training and support. Support is needed in spite of the number of years of experience teachers may have. Change requires a learning curve as new strategies are understood, tested, refined, improved, and adopted. If teachers are not learning new strategies or approaches, what is the purpose of the change?

Inherent Problems

Leaders should have gathered from various chapters that teachers need support in order to make changes in their classroom routines and instructional techniques. Individual teacher evaluations undermine successful implementation when support for change is needed. Why would teachers want to try something new just to be graded down on their attempts? While feedback is necessary for teachers on their performance using a strategy, the feedback needs to encourage continued use of the strategy. Evaluation is needed, but it is program evaluation, not individual teacher evaluation. Individual teachers should not be scored in their early efforts at enacting a new strategy.

Often, it seems that evaluation is the default method for working with teachers. Mathematics coaches, unaccustomed to working with training adults, may have only experienced evaluation during their careers. As a result, when they suddenly find themselves responsible for coaching adults, they resort to the method they have experienced—an evaluative approach. Coaches may assume the job is to enter a classroom, move to the back of the room, observe and record teacher behaviors, and then provide a critique to the teacher. These are the same actions taken by evaluators. Just because teachers have been told that coaches are not evaluating does not mean teachers believe the coaches are not evaluating. After all, they are using the same techniques as their principal. Principals, on the other hand, usually receive training only in evaluation methods. They find it difficult to move between support and evaluation, thus confusing themselves and their teachers.

What Should Leaders Do?

- Analyze the program or initiative in order to identify the critical components present. These critical components make the program work. For instance, if the program requires student collaboration while working on challenging mathematics problems, then various grouping strategies are critical components (pair-share, groups of three or four, and whole group).
- Provide continual training and in-classroom support for use of the critical components.
- Continually gather data concerning both the quantity and quality of the use of the critical components.
- Regularly evaluate the degree of implementation and measureable program results. (Hull, Harbin Miles, & Balka, 2011, p. 37)

Program Culture

Schools have very distinct cultures. Established school and classroom cultures include things such as policies, practices, and procedures. These cultures are reflected in every classroom. In order to work successfully, the program or initiative must work within the parameters. Leaders need to understand that rarely, if indeed ever, does a program or initiative designed to promote change not require actual change to some of the culture. Leaders show great wisdom when they recognize where policies, practices, and procedures conflict with the intended program or initiative.

Inherent Problems

Many times, embedded practices and procedures provide significant impediments to the successful adoption and implementation of a program. Leaders may feel that, because the CCSS are in mathematics, then only mathematics teachers or mathematics classrooms are impacted by the change. This oversight can cause serious problems.

For instance, isolation is a very real impediment to successful adoption of a desired program or initiative. Teaching in isolation is part of a school culture. Isolation has been an embedded culture for so long a period of time that often leaders and teachers are no longer aware it even exists. Isolation is just the way schools operate. Isolation is so deeply embedded that teachers and leaders see classrooms as the sole domain of the teachers and student learning as the lone responsibility of teachers. Isolation is considered as "teacher independence."

Because teachers work in isolation, when new strategies are introduced, they are unsure of both what the strategy looks like in action and what it is supposed to achieve. This means teachers need to collaborate and share. Collaboration and sharing are not part of many school cultures. Changing this culture, and organizing times for mathematics teachers to meet or for mathematics schedules to coincide, can have a ripple effect throughout the school as schedules for other departments are shifted. Furthermore, as isolation is the norm, teachers within the school are unfamiliar with strategies for effective collaborative planning.

Related to this issue is the fact that training and support from traditional professional development frequently do not match the needs of the user. Teachers do not see or experience strategies under real conditions. Another complicating issue is that, as teachers gain experience with components and strategies contained within a program or initiative, they move from novice users to mastery users. To actually gain proficiency and expertise, teachers need different knowledge and skills than they did when first starting implementation of the strategies.

What Should Leaders Do?

- Understand and be able to recognize appropriate uses of critical components of a program or initiative.
- Recognize novice, mastery, and expert levels of usage of the critical components and strategies.

- Be open and unbiased in reviewing school and classroom culture shifts and impediments to change.
- Sustain positive pressure until the program or initiative is fully adopted by all appropriate staff, and the identified need has been addressed. (Hull, Harbin Miles, & Balka, 2011, p. 38)

Change takes positive pressure over time in the form of energy and effort through support and monitoring. If leaders do not exhibit these elements, then teachers have no real expectations to actually change their classroom actions. Without the types of instructional changes discussed in our book, the CCSS content and practices will not be implemented. The formula for change may perhaps best be stated as this:

Adequate Time + Focused Effort = Desired Change

Teachers and leaders must maintain a clear focus on student achievement. The multiple demands created by adopting the CCSS can easily distract from the focus on students. By careful analysis of a recommended program or initiative, leaders and teachers are better prepared to screen programs or initiatives and select ones that have the greatest potential for success.

QUESTIONS FOR DISCUSSION

Given the three screening factors, which appear most problematic to you?

Given your identified problematic factor, what do you recommend be done in the future to resolve the issue?

What are the jobs of designated school leaders in regard to change?

What are the jobs of designated support positions (either official, such as a mathematics specialist, or appointed, such as a leadership team member or department head)?

How can you use information from the book to identify and support change related to the CCSS?

References

Anderson, P., & Brown, A. (2011). *Quality tools for the classroom.* Beech Grove, IN: Beech Grove High School.

Balka, D., Hull, T., & Harbin Miles, R. (2009). *Guide to mathematics leadership: Sequencing instructional change.* Thousand Oaks, CA: Corwin.

Common Core State Standards. (2010). Retrieved January 26, 2012, from www .corestandards.org/the–standards

Hall, G., & Hord, S. (2001). *Implementing change: Patterns, principles, and potholes.* Needham Heights, MA: Allyn and Bacon.

Hull, T., Balka, D., & Harbin Miles, R. (2009). *Guide to mathematics coaching: Processes for increasing student achievement.* Thousand Oaks, CA: Corwin.

Hull, T., Balka, D., & Harbin Miles, R. (2011a). LCM. Retrieved January 26, 2011, from www.mathleadership.com

Hull, T., Balka, D., & Harbin Miles, R. (2011b). *Visible thinking in the K–8 mathematics classroom.* Thousand Oaks, CA: Corwin.

Hull, T., Harbin Miles, R., & Balka, D. (2010). *Overcoming resistance to change: A guide for school leaders and coaches.* Pflugerville, TX: Self-Published.

Hull, T., Harbin Miles, R., & Balka, D. (2011). Overcoming resistance to change: Why isn't it working? *Virginia Mathematics Teacher, 38*(1), 36–38.

Implementation of the Common Core State Standards. (2010). National Council of Teachers of Mathematics Regional Conference presentation. Retrieved January 26, 2012, from http://www.nctm.org/ . . . /Common_Core_Standards/ CCSSM_Grades6–8_120210v.2.ppt

Lotan, R. (2003). Group-Worthy tasks. *Creating Caring Schools 60,* 6(72–75).

Marzano, R. (2003). *What works in schools: Translating research into action.* Alexandria, VA: Association for Supervision and Curriculum Development (ASCD).

National Council of Teachers of Mathematics. (2000). *Principles and standards for school mathematics.* Reston, VA: National Council of Teachers of Mathematics, Inc.

National Council of Teachers of Mathematics. (2011). *Making it happen: A guide to interpreting and implementing common core state standards for mathematics.* Reston, VA: National Council of Teachers of Mathematics, Inc.

National Research Council. (2000). *How people learn: Brain, mind, experience, and school.* Washington, DC: National Academy Press.

National Research Council. (2001). *Adding it up: Helping children learn mathematics.* Washington DC: National Academy Press.

National Research Council. (2004). Engaging schools: fostering high school students' motivation to learn. Washington, DC: National Academy Press.

Reeves, D. (2006). *The learning leader: How to focus school improvement for better results.* Alexandria, VA: Association for Supervision and Curriculum Development (ASCD).

Rogers, E. (1995). *Diffusion of innovations.* New York: The Free Press.

Appendix: Sample Problems Showing CCSS Content and Practices

I t is our hope that teacher teams and leadership teams will find these nine problems useful for initiating conversations about instructional change. The intent of the problem examples is not for teachers to copy and paste the problems into a lesson but to discuss the problems with colleagues while studying the Sequence Chart and Proficiency Matrix. Teacher teams discover that, as students attend to solving challenging problems, better and clearer thinking and reasoning emerge. Provided with appropriate opportunities, students share their reasoning with classroom partners, the teacher, and other students in the classroom. This developmental progress continues until the teachers master a variety of strategies, students attain proficiency on the Standards for Mathematical Practice, collaborative teams function effectively, and leadership teams achieve a critical mass of adopters.

CCSS PROBLEM 1

Grade Level: 1

In problem 1, teachers are using the strategy of pair-share to provide students additional time to reason and reflect on the problem. By working with a partner and sharing individual understandings, students are better prepared to explain their thinking aloud. By using the strategy of showing thinking, teachers are able to assess student understanding. Teachers are also able to provide ongoing formative assessment as they observe, listen, and talk to students.

CCSS Mathematical Practices and Degrees

- 1a. Make sense of problems (Initial).
- 2. Reason abstractly and quantitatively (Initial and INtermediate).

Directions and Strategies

Discuss the idea of collecting objects, and provide some examples such as stamps, coins, dolls, or stuffed toys. Then ask students to share examples. Next, read the problem to the students.

The Problem

Dan's older brother Sam collects car stickers for his scrapbook.

Sam decides to give Dan some of his stickers.

Sam gives Dan 7 stickers.

Sam now has 12 stickers.

How many stickers did Sam have *before* giving some to Dan?

Tell the students:

"With your partner, agree how to solve the problem."

(Use the think-pair-share strategy with a learning partner. Students will individually take a minute to think about a process to solve the problem and then be paired with another student to share ideas together.)

"Be prepared to demonstrate how you solved the problem, and be prepared to explain your thinking."

(Use *Showing Thinking in Classrooms*. Students will demonstrate thinking by explaining their selected solution process.)

Solution and Discussion

Sam had 19 stickers. (Total Stickers – 7 = 12.)

Move around the classroom; observe and listen to students as the problem is being worked. You may observe students working this problem in a variety of ways. For example:

Students may elect to role-play the problem. In this case, they would gather an uncounted number of objects to represent stickers. One student would be Sam and count out 7 stickers (objects) to his or her partner (Dan). Students then count out 12 objects to the student acting as Sam to demonstrate the remaining stickers. Students recognize they need to combine the 7 stickers with the 12 stickers to find the original amount.

Students may decide to select 12 objects that represent the stickers that Sam had after giving 7 stickers to Dan. The students would then count up from 12 (remaining stickers) the 7 stickers (given stickers). Students may do this with objects representing the stickers by counting out 12, then counting out 7, and then counting the number of objects in the pile. These same strategies can be used by drawing representations of stickers.

Some students may actually set up an equation by selecting a symbol (?, X, or box) to represent the original number of stickers. They then show subtracting 7, and that this expression (? – 7) is equal to 12 (? – 7 = 12). Students then perform the operation of adding 7 to 12 and get the answer of 19.

When they have completed working the problem, call on several student pairs to provide their answers to the problem and their method. *(Make sense of problems: Explain their thought processes in solving a problem one way.)* Choose three methods to compare. Then, select two students to role-play, and write two other methods on the whiteboard. *(Reason abstractly and quantitatively: Reason with models or pictorial representations to solve problems.)* As the students enact the problem, point out the numbers contained in the problems, and encourage students to discuss symbolic representations used to indicate the stickers and operations. *(Reason abstractly and quantitatively: Translate situations into symbols for solving problems.)*

CCSS Content

Domain: 1.OA–Operations and Algebraic Thinking

Standard: Represent and solve problems involving addition and subtraction.

Cluster 1: Use addition and subtraction within 20 to solve word problems involving situations of adding to, taking from, putting together, taking apart, and comparing, with unknowns in all positions, for example, by using objects, drawings, and equations with symbols for the unknown numbers to represent the problem.

CCSS PROBLEM 2

Grade Level: 2

In problem 2, students are given a task for which they get to work with partners. The task, while not that challenging, does take collaboration and communication. Students will need to agree on creating and recording numbers. Further, students need to discuss and arrange answers to ensure all possibilities are found. Finally, students will not be allowed to just provide answers. Students will need to explain their reasoning in verifying that all combinations have been found. Students need to learn how to effectively work with partners and small groups.

CCSS Mathematical Practices and Degrees

- 1b. Persevere in solving problems (INtermediate).
- 6. Attend to precision (Initial, INtermediate).

Directions and Strategies

Discuss with students the concept of place value in base ten. Have students identify and name 100s, 10s, and 1s in base ten blocks. Read the problem with the students.

The Problem

There are many three-digit numbers that can be made using any combination of the base ten blocks shown. How many can you find?

100	10	1	1
	10	1	1
	10		

Tell the students:

"With your partner, select one 100, three 10s, and four 1s and place them on your desk. One partner needs to get a sheet of paper and a pencil. Find and record as many three-digit numbers as you can using the place value blocks."

(Use *Initiating Think-Pair-Share.*)

After a reasonable amount of time, when students are engaged and finding answers, ask the students to stop for a moment and share how they are finding answers.

(Use *Showing Thinking in Classrooms.*)

"Now, class, continue working, but this time, I want you to think about how you will know when you have discovered every possible answer. Organize your work so you can explain your thinking."

(Use *Showing Thinking in Classrooms* and *Questioning and Wait Time.*)

Solution and Discussion

There are 20 possible three-digit numbers if teachers allow 0s to be used.

Three-digit numbers require the 100 number block, so for the most part, students are finding combinations with the 10s and 1s. The smallest three-digit number is 100. By counting up, students find:

100; 101; 102; 103; 104

Continuing to count up, students note that they cannot create 105, and so on. The next series begins with 110; 111; 112; 113; 114. Again, students should find they cannot create 115, so the next number series is 120; 121; 122; 123; 124. This is followed by 130; 131; 132; 133; and 134.

Students may try to continue counting up to ensure they are correct but should clearly grasp that, without additional 10s or 1s, no further numbers can be created.

CCSS Content

Domain: 2.NBT—Number and Operations in Base Ten

Standard: Understand place value.

Cluster 1: Understand that the three digits of a three-digit number represent amounts of 100s, 10s, and 1s.

CCSS PROBLEM 3

Grade Level: 2

In problem 3, students are provided a challenging problem to solve with a partner. In this case, students need to critically think about the problem and carefully read and reread the problem. Strategies need to be discussed and agreed upon as students organize their work and seek a solution. As students learn to work with partners, they find it much easier to persevere in finding a solution.

CCSS Mathematical Practices and Degrees

1a. Make sense of problems (INtermediate).

1b. Persevere in solving them (INtermediate).

2. Reason abstractly and quantitatively (Initial).

3a. Construct viable arguments (Initial).

3b. Critique the reasoning of others (Initial).

Directions and Strategies

Provide a variety of coins for pairs of students to work with. Using the think-pair-share strategy, ask students to review combinations of coins that add up to $.50. Some students may want to use a 0–100 number chart to display the combinations. (*Reason abstractly and quantitatively: Reason with models or pictorial representations to solve the problem.*) Have students work with a partner to talk about a process to use with the problem below. (*Make sense of problems* and *persevere in solving them.*) Ask students to share their thinking, demonstrate their solutions, and critique the reasoning of others. (*Construct viable arguments* and *critique reasoning of others.*)

The Problem

"When I emptied my pocket, I found 9 coins, including pennies, nickels, and dimes. The value of my money is 58¢. What coins did I have in my pocket?"

Solution and Discussion

One strategy students may consider is to construct a table using a guess-and-check model. With this model, record each guess, and determine how close the guess is. A good beginning may be to think of 58¢ as 50 + 8. Chart all guesses to determine the correct solution. It is important to remember that the total of all of the coins is 9. Students can adjust the guesses as they get closer to a solution.

Pennies	1	1	2	2	3
Nickels	3	4	3	2	1
Dimes	5	4	4	5	5
Total of Coins	9	9	9	9	9
Possible Amounts	66¢	61¢	57¢	62¢	58¢

CCSS Content

Domain: 2.MD.8—Measurement and Data

Standard: Work with time and money.

Cluster 8: Solve word problems involving dollar bills, quarters, dimes, nickels, and pennies, using $ and ¢ symbols appropriately.

CCSS PROBLEM 4

Grade Level: 3

In problem 3, students are challenged to find the solution to a realistic situation. The students must then take their understanding and translate it into symbolic form. In either form, students need to explain their reasoning and thinking.

CCSS Mathematical Practices and Degrees

- 1a. Make sense of problems (INtermediate).
- 1b. Persevere in solving them (INtermediate).
- 2. Reason abstractly and quantitatively (INtermediate).
- 3a. Construct viable arguments (INtermediate).
- 3b. Critique the reasoning of others (INtermediate).

Directions and Strategies

Talk about allowances and savings to purchase something students want to buy. Share examples with each other. Help students organize thinking with a T-chart (input/output chart). *(Reason abstractly and quantitatively: Reason with models or pictorial representations to solve problems.)* For example, a new CD costs $15.00. A student receives a $3.00 allowance weekly. Week 2 allowance added to week 1 is $6.00, and so on. The T-chart can be filled in as follows:

Weeks	$
1	$3.00
2	$6.00
3	$9.00
4	$12.00
5	$15.00

Have students work with partners to explain their thought processes in solving a problem and representing it in several ways. *(Make sense of problems: Explain their thought processes in solving a problem and representing it in several ways.)* Ask the partners to use appropriate vocabulary and explain to each other why their solutions are correct. Then, allow students to share their thinking, demonstrate their solutions, and critique the reasoning of other children in the classroom. *(Construct viable arguments and critique reasoning of others.)*

The Problem

I am saving my weekly $5.00 allowance to purchase a new digital camera. The camera will cost $45.00. How many weeks will I need to save my allowance? Write an equation with a symbol for the unknown number to represent this problem.

Solution and Discussion

A T-chart (input/output) is easy to complete. Depending on the amount of money needed, an equation may be an easy way to determine the solution to the problem, for example, N × \$5.00 = \$45.00 or \$45 ÷ N = \$5.00. If the amount needed is \$95.00, a T-chart may take time to complete; however, writing an equation with a symbol for the unknown number to represent the problem is a quick way to find a solution.

Weeks	\$
1	\$5.00
2	\$10.00
3	\$15.00
4	?
5	?
6	\$30.00
7	?
8	\$40.00
9	?

CCSS Content

Domain: 3.OA.3—Operations and Algebraic Thinking

Standard: Represent and solve problems involving multiplication and division.

Cluster 3: Use multiplication and division within 100 to solve word problems in situations involving equal groups, arrays, and measurement quantities, for example, by using drawings and equations with symbols for the unknown numbers to represent the problem.

CCSS PROBLEM 5

Grade Level: 3

In problem 5, students are working independently to find solutions to the problems. Conversations and thinking abound when students are then provided the opportunity to explain how they answered the various problems.

CCSS Mathematical Practices and Degrees

- 1a. Make sense of problems (INtermediate).
- 1b. Persevere in solving them (INtermediate).
- 2. Reason abstractly and quantitatively (INtermediate).
- 4. Model with mathematics (INtermediate).

Directions and Strategies

Review and discuss procedures for adding two 2-digit numbers. Distribute a problem sheet similar to the one shown. If possible, distribute number tiles with the digits 3, 4, 5, and 6. Have students read the directions.

The Problem

Use the digits 3, 4, 5, and 6 to complete each number sentence. A digit can only be used once in each number sentence.

$\square\square + \square\square = 108$ $\square\square + \square\square = 99$ $\square\square + \square\square = 90$

$\square\square + \square\square = 81$ $\square\square - \square\square = 31$ $\square\square - \square\square = 18$

Tell students:

"Use your number tiles or paper and pencil to complete the number sentences."

"Record your answers."

"Be prepared to tell me how you solved the problem, not just that the two numbers add up to 108 or they add up to 90. I want you to explain why your answer is correct."

(Use *Showing Thinking in Classrooms*.)

Possible Solutions and Discussion

45 + 63 = 108	64 + 35 = 99	36 + 54 = 90
45 + 36 = 81	34 + 65 = 99	54 − 36 = 18
	65 − 34 = 31	63 − 45 = 18

If students are using number tiles, observe how students place the tiles on the sheet. Focusing on the 1s digit in the sum or difference aids in finding the necessary numbers. To obtain a three-digit sum, a 4 and 6 or 5 and 6 must be in the 10s place. The only way to have 8 as a 1s digit is with 3 and 5. This information leads to 45 + 63. The only way to have 0 as a 1s digit is with 6 and 4. Regrouping must take place. This information leads to 36 + 54. The only way to have 1 as a 1s digit in addition is with 5 and 6. This leads to 45 + 36. There are two ways to get 9 as a 1s digit, 3 and 6 or 4 and 5. This leads to 64 + 35 or 65 + 34. For subtraction, there are three ways to get 1 as a 1s digit 6 – 5, 5 – 4, and 4 – 3. However, only 6 and 3 provide a 10s digit of 3. There are two ways, using regrouping, to get an 8 as a 1s digit, 13 – 5 and 14 – 6. Both cases work in getting a difference of 18.

In moving about the classroom, observe students writing digits in the squares if a pencil is used or placing tiles in the squares. Do they start on the first number sentence because it has a three-digit sum? Did they start on the second number sentence because both digits are in the sum?

Call on students to discuss their thinking. In the first problem, did students consider which digits would produce a three-digit sum? In the second number sentence, did students have different solutions?

To obtain a difference of 18, students need to consider patterns from the basic subtraction table: 13 – 5 = 8 and 14 – 6 = 8.

After discussing student solutions, pose a similar problem using four different consecutive digits such as 5, 6, 7, and 8. Ask students to find the possible sums and differences using the four digits.

CCSS Content

Domain: 3NBT—Number and Operations in Base Ten

Standard: Use place value understanding and properties of operations to perform multi-digit arithmetic.

Cluster 2: Fluently add and subtract within 1,000 using strategies and algorithms based on place value, properties of operations, and the relationship between addition and subtraction.

***

Domain: 3OA—Operations and Algebraic Thinking

Standard: Solve problems involving the four operations, and identify and explain patterns in arithmetic.

(Continued)

(Continued)

Cluster 8: Solve two-step word problems using the four operations. Represent these problems using equations with a letter standing for the unknown quantity. Assess the reasonableness of answers using mental computation and estimation strategies, including rounding.

Cluster 9: Identify arithmetic patterns (including patterns in the addition table or multiplication table), and explain them using properties of operations.

CCSS PROBLEM 6

Grade Level: 4

In problem 6, students need to carefully read the problem for necessary information. They must then decide how to approach the problem so a reasonable solution can be found and they can explain their thinking. Fractions cause students much confusion, especially when the fractions are not in any context for understanding. Once again, teachers are offered the opportunity to assess student knowledge and understanding as they observe, listen, and talk to students.

CCSS Mathematical Practices and Degrees

- 1a. Make sense of problems (INtermediate).
- 1b. Persevere in solving them (INtermediate).
- 2. Reason abstractly and quantitatively (Initial).
- 3a. Construct viable arguments (INtermediate).
- 3b. Critique the reasoning of others (INtermediate).
- 6. Attend to precision (Initial).

Directions and Strategies

Allow students to talk to each other about a process they can use to solve the problem below. (*Make sense of problems* and *persevere in solving them.*) Remind students that organizing thinking helps problem solvers visualize solutions. (*Reason abstractly and quantitatively: Reason with models or pictorial representations to solve problems.*) Charting or making a table is one way to organize the data given in the problem. Tell students to be prepared to demonstrate their thinking and critique the reasoning of other students. (*Critique the reasoning of others: Explain other students' solutions and identify strengths and weaknesses of the solutions* and *construct viable arguments: Explain their own thinking and thinking of others with accurate vocabulary.*)

The Problem

My mom and I like to jog. In 1 hour, my mom can run 6 miles—the time it takes me to run 4 miles. We decided that we would like to run the same distance of 9 miles and finish the race together. How much of a head start do I need for my mom and me to finish together?

Solution and Discussion

Start by using a chart to record how far each person runs in 1 hour. Then, work backward to determine the time spent in $\frac{1}{2}$ hours by dividing each time in half. Using the chart, compute the time for $1\frac{1}{2}$ hours.

Time	Me	My Mom
$\frac{1}{2}$ hour	2	3
1 hour	4	6
$1\frac{1}{2}$ hours	6	9

In $1\frac{1}{2}$ hour, I will cover 6 miles. I need a 3-mile head start to finish with my mom.

CCSS Content

Domain: 4.MD.2—Measurement and Data

Standard: Solve problems involving measurement and conversion of measurements from a larger unit to a smaller unit.

Cluster 2: Use the four operations to solve word problems involving distances, intervals of time, liquid volumes, masses of objects, and money, including problems involving simple fractions or decimals and problems that require expressing measurements given in larger units in terms of smaller units. Represent measurement quantities using diagrams such as number line diagrams that feature a measurement scale.

CCSS PROBLEM 7

Grade Level: 5

In problem 7, students are again working with fractions within a context. They must organize what is given in the problem and then organize what is to be found. Students must come to agreement concerning how the information is to be displayed as well as an approach to solving the problem.

CCSS Mathematical Practices and Degrees

- 1a. Make sense of problems (INtermediate).
- 1b. Persevere in solving them (INtermediate).
- 2. Reason abstractly and quantitatively (Initial).
- 3a. Construct viable arguments (INtermediate).
- 3b. Critique the reasoning of others (INtermediate).
- 6. Attend to precision (Initial).

Directions and Strategies

Provide paper and pencils or manipulative models for students to use in solving the problem.

To solve the problem below, students will need to start with the answer of 2 cookies and should be encouraged to draw pictures as they work backward to find the original amount of cookies. *(Reason abstractly and quantitatively: Reason with models or pictorial representations to solve problems.)*

Have students partner to read the problem and then decide on a strategy and approach to use in solving the problem. *(Make sense of problems* and *persevere in solving them.)* Students will not only share the steps they used but will also explain their reasoning and thinking processes to each other and to the class using pictorial representations. *(Reason abstractly and quantitatively: Reason with models or representations to solve problems.)* Students should be prepared to justify and explain why their solutions are correct and also critique the reasoning of other students. *(Attend to precision: Incorporate appropriate vocabulary and symbols in communicating their reasoning and solution to others.)*

The Problem

> Our class bought cookies for Teacher Appreciation Day. My teacher said she was really hungry and ate $\frac{1}{4}$ of the cookies. Our principal ate $\frac{2}{3}$ of what was left. Then, our music teacher ate $\frac{1}{2}$ of what was left. At the end of the day, our class was told only 2 cookies were left. How many cookies did we bring for Teacher Appreciation Day?

Solution and Discussion

Because you know the amount remaining is 2 cookies, how can you determine how many cookies each teacher and principal ate? Try drawing a model to illustrate the problem. Use the appropriate vocabulary.

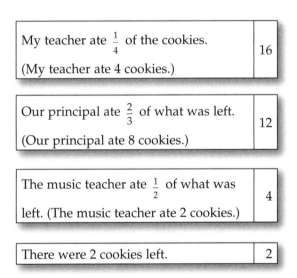

In the final drawing, 2 cookies are left.

Students should be able to explain that the music teacher ate 2 cookies because the same amount is left.

Our principal ate 4 times as much as the music teacher. This gives a total of 12 cookies, which is $\frac{3}{4}$ of the total cookies. If 12 cookies are $\frac{3}{4}$ of the total, then 4 cookies are $\frac{1}{4}$ of the total.

The solution is 16 cookies to start with.

CCSS Content

Domain: 5.NF.2—Number and Operations—Fractions

Standard: Use equivalent fractions as a strategy to add and subtract fractions.

Cluster 2: Solve word problems involving addition and subtraction of fractions referring to the same whole, including cases of unlike denominators, for example, by using visual fraction models or equations to represent the problem. Use benchmark fractions and number sense of fractions to estimate mentally and assess the reasonableness of answers.

CCSS PROBLEM 8

Grade Level: 7

In problem 8, students are working in small groups to solve a challenging problem. Students will need to carefully engage in the mathematics and try several approaches before unlocking all of the possibilities. Through questions and prompts, this problem allows teachers an opportunity to push students' thinking to the advanced degree of proficiency in the practices.

These sample problems highlight instructional strategies and the degrees of proficiency. The intent of the samples is to demonstrate to teachers and leaders that change can be easily initiated by following the sequence of strategy implementation. As students learn to collaborate and gain confidence in sharing aloud their thinking, teachers find it easier to provide students with more challenging problems. This steady cycle of improvement has students attaining the mathematical practices.

CCSS Mathematical Practices and Degrees

- 1a. Make sense of problems (Advanced).
- 2. Reason abstractly and quantitatively (Advanced).
- 3a. Construct viable arguments (Advanced).
- 6. Attend to precision (Advanced).

Directions and Strategies

Have students work in groups of three. Present the problem to students, and provide time for them to read it.

Tell students:

- "In your group, agree how to solve the problem."
- "Be prepared to demonstrate how you solved the problem, and be prepared to explain your thinking and the mathematics that follows that thinking."

(Use *Grouping and Engaging Problems, Allowing Students to Struggle,* and *Encouraging Reasoning.*)

The Problem

Three students guessed the number of jelly beans in a jar. Their guesses were 348, 359, and 368. The guesses were off by 1, 12, and 8 but not in the order of their guesses. How many jelly beans could be in the jar?

Solutions and Discussion

There are two possible solutions: 360 and 352.

While moving around the classroom, listen to students discuss their strategies for solving the problem. Initial attempts might involve just adding 1, 12, and 8 to the appropriate numbers and not considering the direction of the differences:

$348 + 12 = 360, 368 + 12 = 380$

$359 + 1 = 360, 368 + 1 = 369$

$348 + 8 = 356, 359 + 8 = 367$

The information does not indicate whether the guesses were higher or lower than the jelly bean total. In other words, the numbers 1, 12, and 8 represent absolute values. Questions may need to be posed at this point in the problem-solving process for students to understand that different cases must be considered using the three differences.

| 1 and 8 positive, 12 negative | difference of −3 |
| 1 and 8 negative, 12 positive | difference of +3 |

1 and 12 positive, 8 negative	difference of +5
1 and 12 negative, 8 positive	difference of –5
8 and 12 positive, 1 negative	difference of +19
8 and 12 negative, 1 positive	difference of –19
1, 8 and 12 positive	sum of 21
1, 8, and 12 negative	sum of –21

The sum of the three guesses is 1,075. Adding or subtracting each of the above amounts needs to produce a result that is divisible by 3. This is an important point for the groups to understand and explain. If the new result (1,075 plus one of the numbers above) is not divisible by 3, then there would be a fractional part of a jelly bean in the jar.

Adding a difference of 5 gives 1,080, which is divisible by 3. Therefore, there could be 360 jelly beans in the jar.

Subtracting a difference of 19 gives 1,056, which is divisible by 3. Therefore, there could be 352 jelly beans in the jar.

When students have finished solving the problem, have various groups explain their solutions. In many cases, they will find only one solution, 360. If this situation arises, briefly discuss the idea of positive or negative differences.

CCSS Content

Domain: 7NS–The Number System

Standard: Apply and extend previous understandings of operations with fractions to add, subtract, multiply, and divide rational numbers.

Cluster 1b: Understand $p + q$ as the number located a distance $|q|$ from p in the positive or negative direction depending on whether q is positive or negative.

Cluster 1c: Show that the distance between two rational numbers on the number line is the absolute value of their difference, and apply this principle in real-world contexts.

***

Domain: 7EE–Expressions and Equations

Standard: Solve real-life and mathematical problems using numerical and algebraic expressions and equations.

Cluster 3: Solve multistep, real-life mathematical problems posed with positive and negative rational numbers in any form (whole numbers, fractions, and decimals) using tools strategically.

CCSS PROBLEM 9

Grade Level: High School

In problem 9, students are working throughout the eight Standards for Mathematical Practice as well as most of the degrees of proficiency. This problem also provides the classroom teacher the opportunity to effectively utilize all of the recommended strategies from the Sequence Chart. This type of problem provides students and teachers rich opportunities for discussions, reasoning, and justifying. Students are able to compare various solution strategies and approaches. Finally, students learn to persist in finding a solution by learning from prior solution attempts that provided useful information but fell short of finding a solution.

CCSS Mathematical Practices and Degrees

- 1b. Persevere in solving problems (Advanced).
- 2. Reason abstractly and quantitatively (Advanced).
- 3a. Construct viable arguments (Advanced).
- 3b. Critique the reasoning of others (Advanced).
- 4. Model with mathematics (Advanced).
- 8. Look for and express regularity in repeated reasoning (Advanced).

Directions and Strategies

This problem has multiple entry points and involves both algebra and geometry. For algebra, rates of change are important in establishing relationships. If a generalized solution is sought as an extension to the problem, then equations with three variables (angle measure, minutes, hours) are involved. Multiple answers appear. Geometrically, students are dealing with angle measure, a topic that first appears in the CCSS at Grade 4 and then again at Grade 7 in a different context.

Have students work in pairs or groups of three. Present the problem to students, and provide time for them to read it.

The Problem

The angle between the minute hand and the hour hand on a clock is 65°. What time is it?

Tell students:

- "With your partner (s), establish a plan to solve this problem for an angle of 65°."
- "Be prepared to explain your thinking and the mathematics that follows."
- "If you and your partner(s) find an answer, try a different angle measure."

(Use *Grouping and Engaging Problems, Allowing Students to Struggle,* and *Encouraging Reasoning.*)

Teachers monitor the small groups as they work. They are also careful to use wait time. Teachers also allow students to share their solutions, their thinking, and their problem-solving approaches.

Solution and Discussion

There are two solutions: 4:10 and 7:50.

Many students will immediately think about special angle measures on a clock (3:00—90°, 9:00—90°, 6:00—180°). As an entry point, even this information is important because it suggests that there might be more than one time. They will also draw clock faces, attempting to model a 65° angle. This activity in itself will often lead to their reasoning that there is more than one time. (*Model with mathematics: Use a variety of models, symbolic representations, and technology tools to demonstrate a solution to a problem.*)

Another entry point for students is to consider the number of degrees between each of the numbers 1 through 12 on a clock. With 360° in a circle and 12 numbers on the clock, then the angle between any consecutive numbers is $360/12 = 30°$.

With 30° as the angle measure and 5 minutes between each number, then the angle measure between two consecutive minutes is $30/5 = 6°$. (*Reason abstractly and quantitatively: Convert situations into symbols to appropriately solve problems as well as convert symbols into meaningful situations.*)

At this point, many students will move away from the original task and attempt to determine angles for particular times. For example, consider the angle formed at 3:10.

The hour hand has moved toward 4. What is the angle between 3 and the new location at 3:10? It has moved $(10/60)(30) = 5°$. The minute hand is on 2. Therefore, the angle formed is $30° + 5° = 35°$.

In fact, whenever the time is 10 minutes after the hour, the hour hand has moved 5°. Similarly, when the time is 15 minutes after the hour, the hour hand has moved (15/60)(30) = 7.5°. (*Construct viable arguments, and critique the reasoning of others; Compare and contrast various solution strategies, and explain reasoning of others.*)

Although this attempt is fruitful for particular times and requires significant reasoning on the part of students, it does not provide an immediate solution to the original problem.

Students may now reason that there are rates of change important in determining the angles. Consider the rate of change of the angle in degrees per minute. The hour hand moves 360° in 12 hours or 720 minutes. Therefore, it changes at a rate of 360/720 = 0.5° per minute. The minute hand rotates through 360° in 60 minutes. Therefore, it changes at a rate of 360/60 = 6° per minute.

If a clock is on the hour, then the angle measure is a multiple of 30°. For example, at 2:00, the angle is 2(30) = 60°; at 5:00, 5(30) = 150°. If the clock is not on the hour, then the hour hand moves in multiples of 30° plus a part of 30°. That part is determined by the product of the portion of the hour and 30°. For example, at 2:15, the angle formed by the hour hand and 12:00 is 2(30) + 15/60(30) = 60 + 7.5 = 67.5. This generalizes to 30H + (M/60)(30) = 30H + M/2 = (60H + M)/2.

The rate of change of the minute hand is 6° per minute. So, the angle measured clockwise from 12:00 is 6M, where M is the number of minutes.

The angle ß between the two hands can be found using the formula:

$$ß = \left| \left(\tfrac{1}{2} \right)(60H + M) - 6M \right| = \left| \left(\tfrac{1}{2} \right)(60H - 11M) \right|$$

where H is the number of hours and M is the number of minutes.

If ß = 65°, then 65° = $\left| \left(\tfrac{1}{2} \right)(60H - 11M) \right|$, or 130 = |60H − 11M|.

So, 130 = 60H − 11M or − 130 = 60H − 11M.

If H = 4 and M = 10, then ß = 65°. Also, if H = 7 and M = 50, then ß = 65°.

CCSS Content

Domain: A-ERI–Reasoning with Equations and Inequalities

Standard: Understand solving equations as a process of reasoning and explain the reasoning.

Cluster 1: Explain each step in solving a simple equation as following from the equality of numbers asserted at the previous step, starting from the assumption

(Continued)

(Continued)

that the original equation has a solution. Construct a viable argument to justify a solution method.

✳✳✳

Domain: A-SSE—Seeing Structure in Expressions

Standard: Interpret the structure of expressions.

Cluster 1a: Interpret parts of an expression, such as terms, factors, and coefficients.

Cluster 1b: Use the structure of an expression to identify ways to rewrite it.

✳✳✳

Domain: A-CED—Creating Equations

Standard: Create equations that describe numbers or relationships.

Cluster 2: Create equations in two or more variables to represent relationships between quantities; graph equations on coordinate axes with labels and scales.

✳✳✳

Domain: G-MG—Modeling With Geometry

Standard: Apply geometric concepts in modeling situations.

Cluster 1: Use geometric shapes, their measures, and their properties to describe objects.

Index

Note: Page numbers in italics refer to figures.

CORWIN

A SAGE Company

The Corwin logo—a raven striding across an open book—represents the union of courage and learning. Corwin is committed to improving education for all learners by publishing books and other professional development resources for those serving the field of PreK–12 education. By providing practical, hands-on materials, Corwin continues to carry out the promise of its motto: **"Helping Educators Do Their Work Better."**

NATIONAL COUNCIL OF TEACHERS OF MATHEMATICS

The National Council of Teachers of Mathematics is a public voice of mathematics education, supporting teachers to ensure equitable mathematics learning of the highest quality for all students through vision, leadership, professional development, and research.